Lo-Dash Essentials

Implement fast, lean, and readable code effectively with Lo-Dash

Adam Boduch

[PACKT] PUBLISHING open source community experience distilled

BIRMINGHAM - MUMBAI

Lo-Dash Essentials

First published: January 2015

Production reference: 1210115

Published by Packt Publishing Ltd.
Livery Place
35 Livery Street
Birmingham B3 2PB, UK.

ISBN 978-1-78439-833-0

www.packtpub.com

Credits

Author
Adam Boduch

Reviewers
Joe Grund
Richard Hubers
Tyler Morgan
Francois-Guillaume Ribreau
Matt Traynham

Commissioning Editor
Dipika Gaonkar

Acquisition Editor
Meeta Rajani

Content Development Editor
Pooja Nair

Technical Editor
Mrunal M. Chavan

Copy Editors
Vikrant Phadkay
Rashmi Sawant

Project Coordinator
Suzanne Coutinho

Proofreaders
Kevin McGowan
Ameesha Green
Lucy Rowland

Indexers
Priya Sane
Tejal Soni

Production Coordinator
Komal Ramchandani

Cover Work
Komal Ramchandani

About the Author

Adam Boduch is a senior frontend engineer from Toronto. He currently works on delivering innovative products at Virtustream. Adam loves tinkering with the latest JavaScript libraries and is passionate about high-performance user interfaces.

Having focused on writing about jQuery in *jQuery UI Themes Beginner's Guide* and *jQuery UI Cookbook*, both by Packt Publishing, Adam has ventured into a new territory with this title, *Lo-Dash Essentials*. He is an avid proponent of Backbone and the ecosystem that surrounds it.

About the Reviewers

Joe Grund is a full-stack software engineer. He has written numerous rich applications utilizing the latest technologies and methodologies. Joe enjoys writing terse JavaScript code in a functional style and building real-time systems. He works at Intel, where he uses JavaScript to solve interesting problems. He lives in Orlando and can be found on Twitter (`@joegrund`), GitHub (`jgrund`), and his blog (`joegrund.com`), where he muses about building complex systems out of simple functional primitives.

I would like to thank my wife, Sunshine, and my three awesome kids, Luke, Lilly, and Michael, for their love and support.

Richard Hubers is an all-round web developer with more than 15 years of experience. He likes writing web apps and APIs in JavaScript and .NET, and learning the newest and latest technologies. He lives and works in Amsterdam.

Tyler Morgan is a renowned Ruby developer. He loves the JavaScript landscape, especially Node.js. He is an instructor of an intensive full-stack JavaScript development course at Code Fellows, located in Seattle, Washington.

Francois-Guillaume Ribreau is a full-stack developer and French entrepreneur. Currently the CTO of @Bringr and @Redsmin, he also teaches NoSQL, software architecture, JavaScript, and RIA in engineering schools. In his spare time, he reviews books, releases open source libraries (`github.com/FGRibreau`), and shares his discoveries on Twitter (`@FGRibreau`).

Matt Traynham is a Java, JavaScript, and Python developer fascinated by cutting-edge technologies. He has worked on a variety of projects, including but not limited to content management, Big Data, machine learning, statistics, and full-text search. He regularly contributes to his GitHub account at `https://github.com/mtraynham`.

I'd like to thank my wife and best friend, Pamela, who doesn't get mad at me when I'm glued to my laptop.

www.PacktPub.com

Support files, eBooks, discount offers, and more

For support files and downloads related to your book, please visit www.PacktPub.com.

Did you know that Packt offers eBook versions of every book published, with PDF and ePub files available? You can upgrade to the eBook version at www.PacktPub.com and as a print book customer, you are entitled to a discount on the eBook copy. Get in touch with us at service@packtpub.com for more details.

At www.PacktPub.com, you can also read a collection of free technical articles, sign up for a range of free newsletters and receive exclusive discounts and offers on Packt books and eBooks.

PACKTLIB™

https://www2.packtpub.com/books/subscription/packtlib

Do you need instant solutions to your IT questions? PacktLib is Packt's online digital book library. Here, you can search, access, and read Packt's entire library of books.

Why subscribe?

- Fully searchable across every book published by Packt
- Copy and paste, print, and bookmark content
- On demand and accessible via a web browser

Free access for Packt account holders

If you have an account with Packt at www.PacktPub.com, you can use this to access PacktLib today and view 9 entirely free books. Simply use your login credentials for immediate access.

This book is for Melissa, Jason, and Simon. Thanks for all the love and support.

Table of Contents

Preface

At times, JavaScript can be a frustrating programming language to work with. Just when you think you have it entirely figured out, performance or cross-browser issues reveal themselves in the worst possible way. Lo-Dash is just one of many libraries that aim to help JavaScript programmers write code that's elegant, efficient, and portable. Underscore.js introduced a better way to perform functional programming with JavaScript. Lo-Dash is a continuation of this effort, and throughout this book, we'll see what sets Lo-Dash apart from other libraries out there, including Underscore.

At its heart, JavaScript is a functional language, but not necessarily a pure functional language—you can modify variables and introduce side effects. However, functions are first-class citizens and you can do a lot with them. Lo-Dash embraces this idea and gives programmers all the tools they need to write functional code that's readable and maintainable. All the cool things you can do with higher-order functions in other languages are possible with Lo-Dash as well.

It's not just the low-level utilities and performance gains that Lo-Dash delivers, though these are always welcome; it's also the enhanced programming model and the ideas that Lo-Dash borrows from other languages such as functional and applicative programming. These are imparted to JavaScript applications as a coherent API. Underscore got the ball rolling, and Lo-Dash further enhances these ideas, albeit using different design and implementation strategies.

What this book covers

Chapter 1, Working with Arrays and Collections, explains that collections are similar to arrays but are more general than arrays. This chapter looks at the differences between these two constructs and the available Lo-Dash functions that operate on them.

Chapter 2, Working with Objects, teaches you how Lo-Dash treats objects as collections. This chapter looks at the available functions that work with objects.

Chapter 3, Working with Functions, focuses on the functional tools provided by Lo-Dash.

Chapter 4, Transformations Using Map/Reduce, explains that the map/reduce programming model is used often in the Lo-Dash code. This chapter offers many examples that utilize the Lo-Dash map/reduce tools in their various forms.

Chapter 5, Assembling Chains, explains how Lo-Dash can chain together functions that operate on a value. This chapter explores what chains are and how they work.

Chapter 6, Application Building Blocks, looks at the high-level application components that help organize the Lo-Dash code.

Chapter 7, Using Lo-Dash with Other Libraries, explains that Lo-Dash doesn't do everything. This chapter uses examples to illustrate where other libraries can help Lo-Dash and vice versa.

Chapter 8, Internal Design and Performance, looks at some of the internal design decisions of Lo-Dash and provides some advice on how to improve the performance of your Lo-Dash code.

What you need for this book

The only software required for running the examples in this book is a modern web browser. All JavaScript libraries are packaged with the code samples. The only exception is *Chapter 7, Using Lo-Dash with Other Libraries*, which involves working with Node.js (`http://nodejs.org/`) and some corresponding npm packages.

Who this book is for

This book is for the intermediate JavaScript programmer who is either new to Lo-Dash or has been using it for a while. Whether you've never written a line of Lo-Dash or you've got Lo-Dash code running in production, this book has something for you. Ideally, you've written some intermediate/advanced JavaScript code and utilized libraries such as jQuery or Backbone.

Conventions

In this book, you will find a number of styles of text that distinguish between different kinds of information. Here are some examples of these styles, and explanations of their meanings.

Code words in text, database table names, folder names, filenames, file extensions, pathnames, dummy URLs, user input, and Twitter handles are shown as follows: "The `union()` function concatenates collections, with duplicate values removed."

A block of code is set as follows:

```
var collection = [
    { name: 'Jonathan' },
    { first: 'Janet' },
    { name: 'Kevin' },
    { name: 'Ruby' }
];

if (!_.every(collection, 'name')) {
    return 'Missing name property';
}
// → "Missing name property"
```

Any command-line input or output is written as follows:

```
npm install -g grunt-cli grunt-contrib-connect
```

[Warnings or important notes appear in a box like this.]

Reader feedback

Feedback from our readers is always welcome. Let us know what you think about this book—what you liked or may have disliked. Reader feedback is important for us to develop titles that you really get the most out of.

To send us general feedback, simply send an e-mail to `feedback@packtpub.com`, and mention the book title via the subject of your message.

If there is a topic that you have expertise in and you are interested in either writing or contributing to a book, see our author guide on `www.packtpub.com/authors`.

Customer support

Now that you are the proud owner of a Packt book, we have a number of things to help you to get the most from your purchase.

Downloading the example code

You can download the example code files from your account at `http://www.packtpub.com` for all the Packt Publishing books you have purchased. If you purchased this book elsewhere, you can visit `http://www.packtpub.com/support` and register to have the files e-mailed directly to you.

Errata

Although we have taken every care to ensure the accuracy of our content, mistakes do happen. If you find a mistake in one of our books—maybe a mistake in the text or the code—we would be grateful if you could report this to us. By doing so, you can save other readers from frustration and help us improve subsequent versions of this book. If you find any errata, please report them by visiting `http://www.packtpub.com/submit-errata`, selecting your book, clicking on the **Errata Submission Form** link, and entering the details of your errata. Once your errata are verified, your submission will be accepted and the errata will be uploaded to our website or added to any list of existing errata under the Errata section of that title.

To view the previously submitted errata, go to `https://www.packtpub.com/books/content/support` and enter the name of the book in the search field. The required information will appear under the **Errata** section.

Piracy

Piracy of copyrighted material on the Internet is an ongoing problem across all media. At Packt, we take the protection of our copyright and licenses very seriously. If you come across any illegal copies of our works in any form on the Internet, please provide us with the location address or website name immediately so that we can pursue a remedy.

Please contact us at `copyright@packtpub.com` with a link to the suspected pirated material.

We appreciate your help in protecting our authors and our ability to bring you valuable content.

Questions

If you have a problem with any aspect of this book, you can contact us at `questions@packtpub.com`, and we will do our best to address the problem.

1

Working with Arrays and Collections

Lo-Dash offers a wide variety of functions that operate on arrays and collections. This generally involves iterating over the collection in one form or another. Lo-Dash helps make iterative behavior easy to implement, including searching for data, as well as building new data structures.

Collections are at the heart of applicative programming. This is where we will successively apply functions to each element in the collection. This chapter introduces the concept of the collection, something Lo-Dash code uses extensively.

In this chapter, we will cover the following topics:

- Iterating over collections
- Sorting data
- Searching for data
- Slicing collections into smaller pieces
- Transforming collections

The difference between arrays and collections

One of the initial sources of confusion for newcomers to Lo-Dash is the distinction between arrays and collections. The Lo-Dash API has a set of functions for arrays, and a set of functions for collections. But why? It would appear that these functions are interchangeable for any collection. Well, a better definition of what a collection actually is according to Lo-Dash might clear things up.

A collection is an abstract concept. That is, we can use the collection functions found in Lo-Dash on any JavaScript object that we'd like to iterate over. For example, the `forEach()` function will happily iterate over an array, a string, or an object. The subtle differences between these types, and what they mean when it comes to iterating, are hidden from the developer.

The array functions provided by Lo-Dash are less abstract, they do, in fact, expect an array. In a sense, even these functions are abstract because they don't explicitly check for the `Array` type. They require that the object supports numerical indices and that it has a numerical `length` property.

The takeaway is that, in the overwhelming majority of your days as a Lo-Dash programmer, the distinction between arrays and collections does not matter. Mainly, because the primary collection type will be an array anyway. In a small minority of cases, where the distinction does matter, just remember that the array functions have a slightly stricter criteria for what they consider acceptable data.

Iterating over collections

Lo-Dash does a lot of iterating over collections, whether it's done explicitly by the developer, or done implicitly through a higher level Lo-Dash function. Let's take a look at the basic `forEach()` function:

```
var collection = [
    'Lois',
    'Kathryn',
    'Craig',
    'Ryan'
];

_.forEach(collection, function(name) {
    console.log(name);
});
// →
// Lois
// Kathryn
// Craig
// Ryan
```

This code doesn't do much, aside from logging the value of each item in the collection. It does, however, give you a general sense of what iterative functions look like in Lo-Dash. As the name implies, for each element in the array, apply the function callback. There's more than just the current element that's passed to the callback function. We also get the current index.

> **Downloading the example code**
>
> You can download the example code files from your account at `http://www.packtpub.com` for all the Packt Publishing books you have purchased. If you purchased this book elsewhere, you can visit `http://www.packtpub.com/support` and register to have the files e-mailed directly to you.

Take a look at the following code:

```
var collection = [
    'Timothy',
    'Kelly',
    'Julia',
    'Leon'
];

_.forEach(collection, function(name, index) {
    if (name === 'Kelly') {
        console.log('Kelly Index: ' + index);
        return false;
    }
});
// → Kelly Index: 1
```

Returning `false` tells `forEach()` that this iteration will be the last. The index, with each iteration, is incremented and passed to the callback function as the second argument.

The `forEach()` function iterates over the collection in the typical left-to-right fashion. If we want the inverse behavior, we can use the cousin function, `forEachRight()`:

```
var collection = [
    'Carl',
    'Lisa',
    'Raymond',
    'Rita'
];

var result = [];

_.forEachRight(collection, function(name) {
    result.push(name);
});
// →
```

```
// [
//    "Rita",
//    "Raymond",
//    "Lisa",
//    "Carl"
// ]
```

This type of behavior is useful when we're working with sorted collections, as is the case in the preceding code. But, let's say we wanted to render this array data in the DOM in descending order. The preceding code shows that we can render each item in a given iteration. Using the `forEachRight()` function for this scenario has the advantage of not having to reverse-sort the array.

However, many times this shortcut will not suffice, and you have to sort your collections. We'll take a look at the Lo-Dash functions that assist with sorting next.

Sorting data

In Vanilla JavaScript, the approach to sorting involves arrays and two methods. The `sort()` method sorts the array in ascending order, using primitive comparison operations between the items. You can customize this behavior by passing `sort()`, a **comparator** function. For example, you use this callback function to sort an array in descending order. The other method, `reverse()`, simply reverses the order of the array. It's the inverse of the current order, whatever that might be.

The native array `sort()` method sorts the array in-place although you might not want that to happen. Immutable operations reduce side effects because they don't change the original collection. Specifically, you might have requested the API data in a specific order. A region of the UI wants to render this array in a different sort order. Well, you don't want to change the order from what was requested. In this case, it would be better to have a function that returns a new array that contains the items of the original, but in the expected sort order.

Using sortBy()

The `sortBy()` function is the Lo-Dash answer to the native `Array.sort()` method. Since it's an abstract collection function, it's not limited to arrays. Take a look at the following code:

```
_.sortBy('cba').join('');
```

While the function works just fine with strings as the input, the output is a sorted array of characters; hence, the call to join them back together. This is because the `sortBy()` function always returns an array as the result.

The `sortBy()` function is similar to the native `Array.sort()` method, in that it sorts collection items in ascending order by default. Also, similar to the native method, we can pass in a callback function to `sortBy()` that'll customize the sorting behavior, as follows:

```
var collection = [
    { name: 'Moe' },
    { name: 'Seymour' },
    { name: 'Harold' },
    { name: 'Willie' }
];

_.sortBy(collection, function(item) {
    return item.name;
});
```

The preceding callback function passed to `sortBy()` returns the value of an object property. By doing this, the sorting behavior will compare the property values—in this case, `name`—instead of the objects themselves. There's actually a shorter way to achieve the same result:

```
_.sortBy(collection, 'name');
```

This is what's referred to as the **pluck style** shorthand in Lo-Dash terminology. We pass in the name of the property we want to sort the collection by. The value of this property is then plucked from each object in the collection. There's actually a `pluck()` function we'll look at in more depth later on.

The last trick `sortBy()` has up its sleeve takes the pluck shorthand to the next level and allows sorting by multiple property names, as shown in the following code:

```
var collection = [
    { name: 'Clancy', age: 43 },
    { name: 'Edna', age: 32 },
    { name: 'Lisa', age: 10 },
    { name: 'Philip', age: 10 }
];

_.sortBy(collection, [ 'age', 'name' ]);
// →
// [
//   { name: "Lisa", age: 10 },
//   { name: "Philip", age: 10 },
//   { name: "Edna", age: 32 },
//   { name: "Clancy", age: 43 }
// ]
```

The primary determinant of order here is the `age` property. If we specify a second property name, this is used to determine the order of elements that have the same primary sort order. It serves as a tie breaker. Here, there are two objects where `age` equals `10`. Since the `name` property is the secondary sort order, this is how these two objects are sorted. Multiple sort properties is a typical use case in web applications, which would require us to write a surprisingly large amount of JavaScript to achieve, if not for this Lo-Dash utility.

Maintaining the sort order

Using the `sortBy()` function is a great tool for changing the sort order of an existing collection, especially if we don't want to permanently alter the default sort order of that collection. Other times, however, you'll want to permanently keep a collection sorted. Sometimes, this is actually done for us by the backend API that sends us collections in the form of JSON data.

In these situations, sorting is easy because you don't actually have to sort anything. It's already done. The challenge lies in maintaining the sort order. Because, sometimes elements get added to collections in real time. The naive approach to maintain sort order here would be to simply add the new element to the collection then resort it. The Lo-Dash alternative is to figure out the insertion point that will keep the current collection sort order intact. This is shown in the following code:

```
var collection = [
    'Carl',
    'Gary',
    'Luigi',
    'Otto'
];

var name = 'Luke';

collection.splice(_.sortedIndex(collection, name), 0, name);
// →
// [
//     "Carl",
//     "Gary",
//     "Luigi",
//     "Luke",
//     "Otto"
// ]
```

The new `name` variable gets inserted into the second-last position. This is really the only function needed to maintain the order of a sorted collection. The same `splice()` array method is used to remove items from the collection, which doesn't disrupt the order. Adding new items is a challenge because of the search that takes place to figure out the insertion index. The `sortedIndex()` function does a binary search on the collection to figure out where the new item fits.

Searching for data

Applications don't use entire collections. Rather, they iterate over a collection subset, or they look for a specific item in the collection. Lo-Dash has a number of functional tools to help the programmer find the data they need.

Filtering collections

The simplest way to perform a filter operation on a collection using Lo-Dash is to use the `where()` function. This function takes an object argument and will match its properties against each item in the collection, as shown in the following code:

```
var collection = [
    { name: 'Moe', age: 47, gender: 'm' },
    { name: 'Sarah', age: 32, gender: 'f' },
    { name: 'Melissa', age: 32, gender: 'f' },
    { name: 'Dave', age: 32, gender: 'm' }
];

_.where(collection, { age: 32, gender: 'f' });
// →
// [
//   { name: "Sarah", age: 32, gender: "f" },
//   { name: "Melissa", age: 32, gender: "f" }
// ]
```

The preceding code filters the collection on both the `age` and the `gender` properties. The query translates to thirty-two year old females. The `Moe` object matches with neither property, while the `Dave` object matches with the `age` property, but not `gender`. A good way to think about `where()` filtering is that each object property you pass in as the filter will be logical *and* joined together. For example, match the `age` *and* the `gender` properties.

The `where()` function is great for its concise syntax and intuitive application to collections. With this simplicity comes a few limitations. First, the property values that we're comparing to each item in the collection must match exactly. Sometimes, we need comparisons a little more exotic than strict equality. Second, the logical `and` way that `where()` joins query conditions together isn't always desirable. Logical `or` conditions are just as common.

For these types of advanced filtering capabilities, you should turn to the `filter()` function. Here's a basic filter operation that's even simpler than the `where()` queries:

```
var collection = [
    { name: 'Sean', enabled: false },
    { name: 'Joel', enabled: true },
    { name: 'Sue', enabled: false },
    { name: 'Jackie', enabled: true }
];

_.filter(collection, 'enabled');
// →
// [
//   { name: "Joel", enabled: true },
//   { name: "Jackie", enabled: true }
// ]
```

Since the `enabled` property has **truthy** values for two objects in this collection, they're returned in a new array.

> Lo-Dash uses the notion of truthy values everywhere. This simply means that a value will test positive if used in an `if` statement or a ternary operator. Values don't need to be of Boolean type and `true` to be truthy. An object, an array, a string, a number—these are all truthy values. Whereas null, undefined, and 0— are all false.

As mentioned, the `filter()` function fills gaps in the `where()` function. Unlike `where()`,`filter()` accepts a callback function that's applied to each item in the collection, as shown in the following code:

```
var collection = [
    { type: 'shirt', size: 'L' },
    { type: 'pants', size: 'S' },
    { type: 'shirt', size: 'XL' },
    { type: 'pants', size: 'M' }
];

_.filter(collection, function(item) {
```

```
        return item.size === 'L' || item.size === 'M';
});
// →
// [
//   { type: "shirt", size: "L" },
//   { type: "pants", size: "M" }
// ]
```

The callback function uses an `or` condition to satisfy the `size` constraint here—`medium` or `large`. This is simply not doable with the `where` function.

> The `filter()` function accepts an object argument as well. In Lo-Dash terminology, this is called a **where style callback**. There are many functions, not just `filter()`, that accept the filter criteria specified as an object and behave like `where()`.

Filtering collections using the `filter()` function is good when we know what we're looking for. The callback function gives the programmer enough flexibility to compose elaborate criteria. But sometimes, we don't know what you need from a collection. Instead, you only know what you *don't* need, as shown in the following code:

```
var collection = [
    { name: 'Ryan', enabled: true },
    { name: 'Megan', enabled: false },
    { name: 'Trevor', enabled: false },
    { name: 'Patricia', enabled: true }
];

_.reject(collection, { enabled: false });
// →
// [
//   { name: "Ryan", enabled: true },
//   { name: "Patricia", enabled: true }
// ]
```

You can see here that only `enabled` items are returned that are equivalent to doing `_.filter(collection, {enabled: true})`,which is a simple inversion of `filter()`. Which function you use is a matter of personal preference and the context in which they're used. Go for the one that reads cleaner in your code.

> `reject()` actually uses the `filter()` function internally. It uses the `negate()` function to invert the result of the callback passed to `filter()`.

Finding items in collections

Sometimes, we need a specific collection item. Filtering a collection simply generates a new collection with less items in it. Conversely, finding items in a collection means finding a specific item.

The function used to find items in a collection is aptly named `find()`. This function accepts the same arguments as the `filter()` function. You can pass the name of the property as a string, an object filled with property names and values to execute a where style search, or just a plain callback function to match against whatever you want. The following is an example of this:

```
var collection = [
    { name: 'Derek', age: 37 },
    { name: 'Caroline', age: 35 },
    { name: 'Malcolm', age: 37 },
    { name: 'Hazel', age: 62 }
];

_.find(collection, { age:37 });
// → { name: "Derek", age: 37 }
```

There're actually two items matching this where style criteria in the collection—`Derek` and `Malcolm`. If we were to run this code though, we'd see that only `Derek` is returned. That's because `find()` returns as soon as a match is found. Collection order matters when searching for items in collections. It doesn't take into consideration duplicate values.

Let's look in the other direction and see what we find. Using the same collection and the same search criteria, you can search in the opposite direction:

```
_.findLast(collection, { age:37 });
// → { name: "Malcolm", age: 37 }
```

While `find()` searches for the first occurrence of the matching item in the collection, `findLast()` searches for the last occurrence. This is useful when we're working with sorted collections—you can better optimize your linear searches.

> While Lo-Dash heavily optimizes the `while` loops used when iterating over collections, searches executed using functions such as `find()` are linear. It's important to remember that it's up to the programmer using Lo-Dash to consider the performance implications of their unique application data. Lo-Dash functions are optimized for the generic common case, they're not going to magically make your code faster by virtue of using them. They're tools to *assist* the programmer to make incredibly high-performance code.

Slicing collections into smaller pieces

So far we've seen how collections can be filtered, creating a new smaller collection. Lo-Dash supplies you with a number of functions that take existing arrays and produce one or more smaller arrays. For example, you might want a portion of the first part of any array—or a portion of the last part. Arrays can be divided into chunks of smaller arrays that are useful for batched processing. You can also use Lo-Dash array tools to remove duplicates, thus ensuring the uniqueness of your array.

First and last collection portions

With native JavaScript arrays, you can slice off the first portion of an array using the `slice()` array method. Lo-Dash provides abstractions on top of the native array `slice()` method that make it a little easier for the developer to write intuitive code—this isn't always the case with the native array approach. Further, the Lo-Dash `take()` function operates on collections, so it'll work with both arrays and strings, as shown in the following code:

```
var array = [
    'Steve',
    'Michelle',
    'Rebecca',
    'Alan'
];

_.take(array, 2);
// → [ "Steve", "Michelle" ]

_.take('lodash', 2).join('');
// → "lo"
```

There's a difference in the output when using `take()` on arrays and strings. When applying it to an array, it generates a new array, a subset of the original. However, when applying `take()` to strings, it returns a new array of individual characters. The preceding code will return `[ 'l', 'o' ]`. That's probably not what we're after most of the time, so we'll just join these characters back together with an empty string.

We can slice off the last portions of collections and strings using the `takeRight()` function. Using the same array and string, you can run the following code to get the last portions of the collections:

```
_.takeRight(array, 2);
_.takeRight(string, 4).join('');
```

The resulting array looks like `[ 'Rebecca', 'Alan']`. The resulting string looks like `'dash'`.

Applying `take()` to a collection without any arguments will slice the first item. Likewise, applying `takeRight()` without any arguments slices off the last item. In both the cases, the returned value is a one item array, not the item itself. If you're just after the first or last collection items, use the `first()` and `last()` Lo-Dash functions respectively.

Splitting collections into chunks

Sometimes, we're faced with large collections. Really large collections. Especially when using API data, the frontend doesn't always have control over the size of the dataset that's returned. When the API does return a mountain of data, there's a good chance that our code that processes it will lock the UI. We can't exactly say give me less data to work with so that the UI doesn't freeze. Freezing the UI is also unacceptable.

Lo-Dash iterates through collections very efficiently. It doesn't, however, have any control over the potentially expensive operations carried out by your code. And this is what causes the UI to freeze - not the size of the collection by itself, and not by executing an expensive operation once - it's the two factors combined together that become lethal for UI responsiveness.

The `chunk()` function is an easy way to split the processing of a really large collection into several smaller tasks. This gives the chance for the UI to update—render the pending DOM updates and processes the pending events. The usage of this function can be seen in the following code:

```
function process(chunks, index) {
    var chunk = chunks[index];
    if (_.isUndefined(chunk)) {
        return;
    };
    console.log('doing expensive work ' + _.last(chunk));
    _.defer(_.partial(process, chunks, ++index));
}

var collection = _.range(10000),
    chunks = _.chunk(collection, 50);

process(chunks, 0);
// →
// doing expensive work 49
// doing expensive work 99
// doing expensive work 149
```

If the preceding code is a bit of a turn off, don't worry. There're a few new concepts introduced here that you might find confusing. Let's start by explaining at a high level what the code is actually doing. A large collection is created and it's split into chunks of smaller collections. The `process()` function does some work with each chunk, then calls itself again to process the next chunk, until there are no chunks left.

The collection itself is generated using the `range()` function, with `10000` integers in it. It's not the content that's important, but rather, the large size. The `chunk()` function is used to split the large collection into smaller ones. We specify the size we want each chunked collection to be and in this case, we get 20 smaller collections with 50 items each. The processing work is kicked off by the call to `process(chunks, 0)`. The second argument is the first chunk to begin with.

The `process()` function itself grabs the next chunk to process based on the `index` argument. If the chunk is undefined, it means that the end has been reached and there are no more chunks to process. Otherwise, we can start doing expensive processing on the chunk, as illustrated in the example with the `console.log()` call. Finally, the `defer()` function will start processing the next chunk. The reason we're using `defer()` is so that the call stack has a chance to clear, and the DOM operations have a chance to run. If we don't do this, there wouldn't be any point in using `chunk()` to split the processing. The `defer()` function expects a callback, and we make one using `partial()`, which creates a new function, with arguments already supplied to it.

> The `defer()` and `partial()` functions are covered in much more depth in *Chapter 3, Working with Functions*.

How do we know what size to make our array chunks? In the previous code, we chose `50` as the chunk size. But is that an arbitrary decision, or is it based on the typical datasets used in the application? The short answer is that we have to tinker a little and optimize for the common case. This might mean doing something such as figuring out the chunk size based on a percentage of the overall collection size, as shown in the following code:

```
var collection = _.range(10),
    size = Math.ceil(0.25 * collection.length);
_.chunk(collection, size);
// →
// [
//   [ 0, 1, 2 ],
//   [ 3, 4, 5 ],
//   [ 6, 7, 8 ],
//   [ 9 ]
// ]
```

The chunk size here turns out to be `3`. The actual size is 2.5, but you take the ceiling of that since there's no such thing as 2.5 collection elements. Besides, what you're interested in is not the exactness of the chunk size, but rather, the proximity to the 25 percent.

> You might have noticed that `3` doesn't divide evenly into 10. The `chunk()` function is smart enough to not leave out items. Any remaining items that do not fill the chunk size are still included.

Building unique arrays

Collections sometimes have unwanted duplicates in them. This could be a result of the API data itself that contains the duplicates, or as a side effect of other computations you're performing in the frontend. Regardless of the cause, Lo-Dash provides the tools necessary to quickly generate unique collections.

The `uniq()` function takes a collection as the input and generates a new collection as output, with any duplicates removed:

```
var collection = [
    'Walter',
    'Brenda',
    'Arthur',
    'Walter'
];

_.uniq(collection);
// → [ "Walter", "Brenda", "Arthur" ]
```

By default, the potential duplicates are compared against one another using the strict equality operator. In the preceding collection, the duplicate is found and removed because of `'Walter' === 'Walter'`. You can specify, in more detail, how you want `uniq()` to compare values. For example, if we had a collection of objects and we only want unique objects based on the `name` property, we could write `_.uniq(collection, 'name')`. The function also accepts a callback, which is used to compute the values before they're compared. This is useful in situations where the uniqueness of an object isn't so straightforward, as in the following code:

```
var collection = [
    { first: 'Julie', last: 'Sanders' },
    { first: 'Craig', last: 'Scott' },
    { first: 'Catherine', last: 'Stewart' },
```

```
    { first: 'Julie', last: 'Sanders' },
    { first: 'Craig', last: 'Scott' },
    { first: 'Janet', last: 'Jenkins' }
];

_.uniq(collection, function(item) {
    return item.first + item.last;
});
// →
// [
//   { first: "Julie", last: "Sanders" },
//   { first: "Craig", last: "Scott" },
//   { first: "Catherine", last: "Stewart" },
//   { first: "Janet", last: "Jenkins" }
// ]
```

This code ensures that the uniqueness of each object in the collection is based on the full name. There's no full name property, perhaps it's not needed anywhere else in the application. So, the `uniq()` function can just construct one on-the-fly, which is used for the sole purpose of validating this constraint.

Transforming collections

Lo-Dash has a number of tools for transforming collections into new data structures. Additionally, there are tools that can take two or more collections and combine them into a single collection. These functions focus on the most common, yet most burdensome programming tasks faced by frontend developers. Instead of focusing on boilerplate collection transformations, you can get back to making a great application—users don't care about awesome compact code as much as you do.

Grouping collection items

Items in collections are sometimes grouped implicitly. For example, let's say there's a `size` property for a given class of objects whose allowable values are `'S'`, `'M'`, or `'L'`. The code in your frontend application might need to round up the items that contain these various groups for display purposes. Rather than writing our own code, we'll let the `groupBy()` function handle the intricacies of constructing such a grouping:

```
var collection = [
    { name: 'Lori', size: 'S' },
    { name: 'Johnny', size: 'M' },
```

```
        { name: 'Theresa', size: 'S' },
        { name: 'Christine', size: 'S' }
    ];

    _.groupBy(collection, 'size');
    // →
    // {
    //   S: [
    //     { name: "Lori", size: "S" },
    //     { name: "Theresa", size: "S" },
    //     { name: "Christine", size: "S" }
    //   ],
    //   M: [
    //     { name: "Johnny", size: "M" }
    //   ]
    // }
```

The `groupBy()` function, as you might have noticed by now, doesn't return a collection—it takes a collection as the input, but transforms it into an object. This object that `groupBy()` returns contains the original items of the input collection, they're just organized differently. The properties of the object are the values you want to group by. A majority of collection items in the preceding code will reside in the `S` property.

> You'll also see that transformative functions such as `groupBy()` don't actually modify the items themselves—just the collections they're in. That's why, in the resulting object from the preceding code, each item still has its `size` property, despite not really being needed.

When you pass in the property name as a string, `groupBy()` will use a pluck style callback to grab the value of that property from each item in the collection. The unique property values form the keys of the group object. As is often the case, object properties aren't clear-cut and need to be computed at runtime. In the context of grouping items, function callbacks can be used to group collection items in cases where grouping isn't a matter of a simple comparison, as in the following code:

```
var collection = [
    { name: 'Andrea', age: 20 },
    { name: 'Larry', age: 50 },
    { name: 'Beverly', age: 67 },
    { name: 'Diana', age: 39 }
];

_.groupBy(collection, function(item) {
```

```
    return item.age > 65 ? 'retired' : 'working';
});
// →
// {
//   working: [
//     { name: "Andrea", age: 20 },
//     { name: "Larry", age: 50 },
//     { name: "Diana", age: 39 }
//   ],
//   retired: [
//     { name: "Beverly", age: 67 }
//   ]
// }
```

Rather than test for equality, this callback function tests for approximations. That is, anything greater than `65` in the `age` property is assumed to be retired. And we return that string as the group label. Keep in mind that it's best if these callback functions return primitive types for the keys. For any other values, the string `working` is returned. What's nice about these callback functions is that they can be used to quickly generate reports on the API data you're working with. The preceding example illustrates this with a one-liner callback function passed to `groupBy()`.

> Although the `groupBy()` function will accept a where style object as the second parameter, this might not be what you're after. For example, if an item in the collection passes the test, it'll end up in the `true` group. Otherwise, it's a part of the `false` group. Be careful before going too far down the road with a pluck or where style callback—they might not do what you expect. Fiddle around and get quick results to sanity check your approach.

Counting collection items

Lo-Dash helps us find the minimum and maximum values of a collection. We might not need any help if we're working with a lot of arrays that contain only numbers. If that's the case, `Math.min()` is our friend. In nearly any other scenario, the `min()` and `max()` functions are the way to go, if for no other reason than the callback support. Let's take a look at the following example:

```
var collection = [
    { name: 'Douglas', age: 52, experience: 5 },
    { name: 'Karen', age: 36, experience: 22 },
    { name: 'Mark', age: 28, experience: 6 },
```

```
    { name: 'Richard', : age: 30, experience: 16 }
];

_.min(collection, 'age'),
// → { name: "Mark", age: 28, experience: 6 }

_.max(collection, function(item) {
    return item.age + item.experience;
});
// → { name: "Karen", age: 36, experience: 22 }
```

The first call is to `min()` and it gets a string argument—the name of the property we want the minimum value of in the collection. This uses the pluck style callback shorthand and produces concise code where you know the property you're working with. The second call in the preceding code is to `max()`. This function supports the same callback shorthand as `min()`, but here, there's no pre-existing property value for you to work with. Since what you want is the `age` property plus the `experience` property, the callback function supplied to `max()` computes this for us and figures out the maximum.

Note that the `min()` and `max()` functions return the actual collection item and not the minimum or maximum value. This makes sense because we're probably going to want to do something with the item itself, and not just the min/max value.

Beyond locating the minimum and maximum values of collections is finding the actual size of collections. This is easy if you're working with arrays because they already have the built-in `length` property. It is the same with strings. However, objects don't always have a `length` property. The Lo-Dash `size()` function tells you how many keys an object has, which is the intuitive behavior you'd expect from an object, but isn't there, by default. Take a look at the following code:

```
var collection = [
    { name: 'Gloria' },
    { name: 'Janice' },
    { name: 'Kathryn' },
    { name: 'Roger' }
];

var first = _.first(collection);
_.size(collection); // → 4
_.size(first); // → 1
_.size(first.name); // → 6
```

The first call to `size()` returns the length of the collection. It'll look for a `length` property, and if the collection has one, this is the value that's returned. Since it's an array, the `length` property exists, and has a value of `4`. This is what's returned. The `first` variable is an object, so it has no `length` property. It'll count the number of keys in the object and return this value—in this case, `1`. Lastly, `size()` is called on a string. This has a length value of `6`.

We can see from all three uses of `size()` that there's little guessing involved. Where the default JavaScript behavior is inconsistent and unintuitive, Lo-Dash provides a single function to address common use cases.

Flattening and compacting

Arrays can nest to arbitrary depth and sometimes contain falsey values that are of no practical use. Lo-Dash has functions to deal with both these situations. For example, a component of our UI might get passed as an array that has arrays nested inside it. But our component doesn't make use of this structure, and it's, in fact, more of a hindrance than it is helpful. We can *flatten* the array to extract and throw away the unnecessary structure your component does not need, as shown in the following code:

```
var collection = [
    { employer: 'Lodash', employees: [
        { name: 'Barbara' },
        { name: 'Patrick' },
        { name: 'Eugene' }
    ]},
    { employer: 'Backbone', employees: [
        { name: 'Patricia' },
        { name: 'Lillian' },
        { name: 'Jeremy' }
    ]},
    { employer: 'Underscore', employees: [
        { name: 'Timothy' },
        { name: 'Bruce' },
        { name: 'Fred' }
    ]}
];
var employees = _.flatten(_.pluck(collection, 'employees'));

_.filter(employees, function(employee) {
```

```
        return (/^[bp]/i).test(employee.name);
});
// →
// [
//    { name: "Barbara" },
//    { name: "Patrick" },
//    { name: "Patricia" },
//    { name: "Bruce" }
// ]
```

Of course, we don't actually alter the structure of the original collection, we build a new one on the fly, better suited for the current context. In the preceding example, the collection consists of `employer` objects. However, our component is more concerned with the `employee` objects. So, the first step is to pluck those out of their objects using `pluck()`. This gets us an array of arrays. Because what we're actually plucking is the `employee` array from each `employer` array.

The next step is to flatten this `employee` array into an array of `employee` objects, which `flatten()` handles easily. The point of doing all this, which isn't really a lot, is now we have an easy structure to filter. Particularly, this code uses the flattened collection structure to filter out the employee names that start with `b` or `p`.

> There's another flatten function called `flattenDeep()`, which goes to arbitrary nested array depths to create a flattened structure. This is handy when you need to go beyond the one level of nesting that `flatten()` looks in. However, it's not a good idea to flatten arrays of unknown size and depth, simply due to the performance implications. There's a good chance that large array structures can lock the UI for your users.

A close cousin to `flatten()` is the `compact()` function, often used in conjunction with one another. We'll use `compact()` to remove the falsey values from a flattened array, to just use it on a plain array that already exists, or just to take out the falsey values before it's filtered. This is shown in the following code:

```
var collection = [
    { name: 'Sandra' },
    0,
    { name: 'Brandon' },
    null,
    { name: 'Denise' },
    undefined,
    { name: 'Jack' }
    ];
```

```
var letters = [ 's', 'd' ],
    compact = _.compact(collection),
    result = [];

_.each(letters, function(letter) {
    result = result.concat(
        _.filter(compact, function(item) {
            return _.startsWith(item.name.toLowerCase(), letter);
        })
    );
});
// →
// [
//   { name: "Sandra" },
//   { name: "Denise" }
// ]
```

We can see that this collection has some values in it that we clearly don't want to deal with. But, the hopefully-not-so-sad reality is that doing frontend development in a dynamically-typed language with backend data means that you have no control over a lot of sanity checking. All that the preceding code does with the `compact()` function is remove any of the falsey values from the collection. These are things such as `0`, `null`, and `undefined`. In fact, this code wouldn't even run without compacting the collection since it makes the implicit assumption about the `name` property being defined on each object in the collection.

Not only can `compact()` be used for safety purposes—removing items that violate contracts—but also for performance purposes. You'll see that the preceding code searches the collection, *inside* a loop. Therefore, any items removed from the collection *before* the outer loop is entered, the greater the performance gain.

Going back to the preceding code, there's one issue that can catch Lo-Dash programmers off guard. Let's say that we don't want anything that doesn't have a `name` property. Well, we're only shaving off falsey values—objects without `name` properties are still valid, and the `compact()` function lets them through. For example, {} doesn't have a `name` property, and neither does `2`, but they're both allowed through in the previous approach. A safer approach might be to pluck then compact, as shown in the following code:

```
var collection = [
    { name: 'Sandra' },
    {},
    { name: 'Brandon' },
    true,
```

```
        { name: 'Denise' },
        1,
        { name: 'Jack' }
        ];
var letters = [ 's', 'd' ],
    names = _.compact(_.pluck(collection, 'name')),
    result = [];

_.each(letters, function(letter) {
    result = result.concat(
        _.filter(names, function(name) {
            return _.startsWith(name.toLowerCase(),
                                letter);
        })
    );
});
```

Here, we're faced with a similar filtering task but with a slightly different collection. It has objects that will cause our code to fail because they don't have a name key with a string value. The quick-and-dirty workaround is to pluck the `name` property from all items in the collection before performing the `compact()` call. This will yield undefined values for objects that don't have a `name` property. But that's exactly what we're after, since `compact()` has no trouble excluding these values. Moreover, our code is actually simpler now. The caveat being, sometimes the simple approach doesn't work. Sometimes, you need the full object and not just the name. Cheat only when you can get away with it.

Validating some or all items

Sometimes, sections of our code hinge on the validity of all, or some collection items. Lo-Dash provides you with two complementary tools for the job. The `every()` function returns `true` if the callback returns `true` for every item in the collection. The `some()` function is a lazy brother of `every()` – it gives and returns `true` as soon as the callback returns `true` for an item, as shown in the following code:

```
var collection = [
    { name: 'Jonathan' },
    { first: 'Janet' },
    { name: 'Kevin' },
    { name: 'Ruby' }
];

if (!_.every(collection, 'name')) {
```

```
        return 'Missing name property';
}
// → "Missing name property"
```

This code checks every item in the collection for a `name` property before doing anything with it. Since one of the items is using an incorrect property name, the code will return early. The code that runs below the `if` statement can assume that each item has a `name` property.

On the other hand, we might only want to know whether *any* items have a necessary value. You can use this technique to greatly increase performance. For example, say that you have a loop that performs expensive operations on each collection item. You can do a **preflight check**, which is relatively inexpensive, to determine whether the expensive loop is worth running. An example for this is as follows:

```
var collection = [
    { name: 'Sean' },
    { name: 'Aaron' },
    { name: 'Jason' },
    { name: 'Lisa' }
];
if (_.some(collection, 'name')) {
    // Perform expensive processing...
}
```

If the `some()` call makes it all the way through the collection without any `true` callback return values, it means that we can skip the more expensive processing. For example, if we have a potentially large collection and we need to filter it using some nontrivial comparison operators, perhaps some function calls as well, the overhead really starts to add up. Using `some()` is a cheap way to avoid this heavy processing if it's needless.

Unions, intersections, and differences

The last section of this chapter looks at Lo-Dash functions that compare two or more arrays and yield a resulting array. In a way, we're combining several collections into a single collection. The `union()` function concatenates collections, with duplicate values removed. The `intersection()` function builds a collection with values common to all the provided collections. Lastly, the `xor()` function builds a collection that contains the differences between all provided collections. It's kind of like the inverse of `intersection()`.

You can use the `union()` function when there are several overlapping collections that contain similar items—possibly the same items. Rather than iterate through each collection individually, it's easier to combine the collections, while at the same time removing duplicates, as you can see in the following code:

```
var css = [
    'Philip',
    'Donald',
    'Mark'
];
var sass = [
    'Gary',
    'Michelle',
    'Philip'
];
var less = [
    'Wayne',
    'Ruth',
    'Michelle'
];

_.union(css, sass, less);
// →
// [
//   "Philip",
//   "Donald",
//   "Mark",
//   "Gary",
//   "Michelle",
//   "Wayne",
//   "Ruth"
// ]
```

This code takes three arrays and transforms them into a single array. You can see in the resulting array that there's no overlap. That is, any items that exist in more than one of the input arrays are only included in the resulting array once. Let's see what the overlap looks like using `intersection()`:

```
var css = [
    'Rachel',
    'Denise',
    'Ernest'
];

var sass = [
```

```
    'Lisa',
    'Ernest',
    'Rachel'
];

var less = [
    'Ernest',
    'Rachel',
    'William'
];

_.intersection(css, sass, less);
// → [ "Rachel", "Ernest" ]
```

Here, the intersection is `Ernest` and `Rachel`, since these strings exist in all three collections that were passed into `intersection()`. Now it's time to look at comparing the differences between two collections using `xor()`:

```
var sass = [
    'Lisa',
    'Ernest',
    'Rachel'
];
var less = [
    'Ernest',
    'Rachel',
    'William'
];

return _.xor(sass, less);
// → [ "Lisa", "William" ]
```

Passing these two arrays to `xor()` will generate a new array that contains the difference between the two. In this case, the difference is `Lisa` and `William`. Everything else is the intersection.

> The `xor()` function accepts an arbitrary number of collections to compare with. Exercise caution, however, when comparing more than two collections. The most common case is to compare two collections to figure out the difference between the two. Going beyond that is venturing into set theory, and you might not get the results you'd expect.

Summary

This chapter introduced you to the concept of a collection and how they can be compared to arrays. Lo-Dash treats collections as an abstract concept—all JavaScript arrays are collections, but not all collections are arrays. We were introduced to the concept of iterating over collections using the tools provided by Lo-Dash—a fundamental concept in applicative programming and will be touched upon frequently throughout this book.

Collections can be filtered and items can be fetched from the collection. Lo-Dash also gives you the tools needed to transform collections into other structures you need when implementing frontend UI components.

We've been given a taste of some common themes in Lo-Dash programming—like the idea that callback functions are central to almost everything, and the various shorthands that can save on coding effort, such as the pluck and where callbacks. Now it's time to look at how Lo-Dash works with objects, and the various functions at our disposal there, which will be covered in the next chapter.

2

Working with Objects

Everything in JavaScript is an object. This includes functions, arrays, and strings. There's also the notion of a plain object—a dictionary of key-value pairs. This latter structure is useful when you need support with looking up values by a key. In other words, something that a programmer would likely want to read—instead of a numerical index found in arrays.

Lots of APIs return JSON data—you'll often find plain objects. While you can achieve much using JavaScript objects on their own, Lo-Dash makes life easier for doing common things with objects. These functions make the mundane a little less boring as you'll soon find out, you can often find a less verbose approach to working with objects.

In addition to plain object access and manipulation, Lo-Dash has several utility functions that can be applied to any object in your code. These are mostly concerned with validating the type of object you're working with, a duplicitous task using Vanilla JavaScript.

In this chapter, we will cover the following topics:

- Determining an object type
- Assigning and accessing properties
- Iterating over objects
- Calling methods
- Transforming objects
- Creating and cloning objects

Determining an object type

In this section, we'll look at how type validation is typically handled in JavaScript and how the type-checking functions in Lo-Dash improve the situation.

Type coercion

Type coercion happens in JavaScript when one object is compared to another. That is, we have one object operand, the operator, and the second object operand. Depending on the operation being performed, the second object might be coerced into a representation that is compatible with the first operand. Take the following operation, for example:

```
true == 1
```

These are obviously different objects representing different primitive types. In the spirit of loosely typed programming, this expression triggers type coercion. The first operator is a Boolean value and the second operator is a number. The `==` equality operator will take the Boolean representation of `1` and compare it with `true`. This is why, this expression always evaluates to `true`. The values are *roughly* equal.

You can avoid type coercion using the strict equality operator. The following expression will evaluate to `false` since the two operators are compared in their raw forms:

```
true === 1
```

So why turn off type coercion? This seems like a useful tool. Well, it's useful when you don't care about certain things. For example, the previous chapter introduced you to the concept of truthy and falsey values—things that are roughly true or are roughly false. Here, type coercion is your friend because it captures a range of possible values, instead of having to strictly check for equality for a number of possible values. In short, type coercion exists to make your life easier by writing less code.

There are times, however, where type coercion doesn't help at all, and can instead introduce insidious bugs that are painful to track down. For example, let's negate some values with the following expressions:

```
!false;
!undefined;
!0;
```

These all evaluate to `true` and this fact can be problematic to our code. Especially, the fact that an object can have a missing property, and this will evaluate to the same thing as a defined property with a `false` or `0` value. Again, it helps you to be explicit in these scenarios and turn off type coercion using the strict equality/inequality operator.

So, what's the point of all this and what does it have to do with Lo-Dash? The preceding expressions are just a small sampling of the literally thousands of edge cases and issues that can come about when different types of objects interact in our application. Lo-Dash aims to reduce some of these complexities by providing consistent behavior. Internally, Lo-Dash has to perform all kinds of ugly type comparisons and checks so that we don't have to perform them. As an added bonus, these utility functions are exposed in the Lo-Dash API.

Managing function arguments

It's not always clear what kind of arguments our functions will be called with. Nor is it enforced that the number of arguments specified in our function declaration match the number supplied by the caller—these are called **variadic** functions. The type-checking facility provided by Lo-Dash can better prepare your functions to handle anything that's thrown in their way.

For example, you can explicitly check each function argument in order to determine what's being passed to your function. In the case of optional arguments, you can use these functions to explicitly check whether anything was passed as an argument at all, as shown in the following code:

```
function hello(name) {
    if (_.isString(name)) {
        return 'hello, ' + name;
    }
}

hello('world');
// → "hello, world"

hello();
// → undefined
```

If the `name` parameter isn't a string, it isn't anything else, in other words, the function does nothing. This is the case in the preceding code, in the second call to `hello()`. Rather than doing nothing, we can have some other recourse built into your function, but that's specific to what our function does. The point is that we're conscientious of what might get passed our way.

A variation on whether an argument is present or not, in a function call, is the order in which the arguments are passed. You can ignore the last parameter because its value is undefined and it's optional anyway. However, what if our function takes three parameters and the second one is optional? We have to juggle the arguments and their values inside our function. A lot of libraries do this and Lo-Dash simplifies matters with its type-checking functions, as shown in the following code:

```
function hello(greeting, person) {
    if (_.isPlainObject(greeting)) {
        person = greeting;
        greeting = 'hi, ';
    }
    return greeting + person.name;
}

hello('hello, ', { name: 'Dillan' });
// → "hello, Dillan"

hello({ name: 'Danielle' });
// → "hi, Danielle"
```

Here, the `hello()` function expects a `greeting` string and a `person` object. It turns out that the `greeting` parameter is actually optional but it's the first parameter. So the function checks whether `greeting` is actually a plain object, signaling that the `greeting` string was omitted. Then, you just make sure that `person` is assigned the value of `greeting`.

> All these type-checking operations can actually be done using Vanilla JavaScript. On the other hand, there are nuances to doing this because of JavaScript's esoteric type system. Lo-Dash just takes the common things that you don't have to check yourself and exposes them as easy-to-decipher function names.

Arithmetic

If you've ever done arithmetic in your JavaScript application, you know that using the wrong types as operands can lead to some truly puzzling results. For example, the following expressions might or might not look familiar:

```
1/0; // Infinity
1+'one'; // NaN
```

The gist of the matter is that when these guys rear their heads, it's generally not a good sign. This can happen as a result of our own function code (under heavy development and not in production, obviously) or it would just be that our function is getting called with bad data. In either scenario, we need to be prepared to troubleshoot what's happening. We do this by providing a safety net for our arithmetical operations, as shown:

```
var operand1 = 1/0,
    operand2 = NaN,
    results = [];

_.forEach([ operand1, operand2 ], function(op) {
    if (_.isFinite(op)) {
        results.push('operand 1 is finite');
    } else {
        if (!_.isNumber(op) || _.isNaN(op)) {
            results.push(op.toString() + ' is not a number');
        } else {
            results.push('Infinity cannot be used here');
        }
    }
});

return results;
// →
// [
//   "Infinity cannot be used here",
//   "NaN is not a number"
// ]
```

This code iterates over the operands and checks whether each operand is finite using the `isFinite()` Lo-Dash function. This function can be thought of as a catch-all; if this test passes, then you're generally safe to perform arithmetic using the operand. The `else` code runs if `isFinite()` fails, and it's an attempt to find a reason for the failure. If it's not a number, then it's obviously not finite. This will include values such as `true`, `String`, or `null`. On the other hand, if it is a number that's not finite, we know that we're dealing with infinity.

> `NaN` is actually a number—the JavaScript type system at its best. That's why the `if` statement in the preceding code has a check for `!_.isNumber()` or `_.isNaN()`.

Callable objects

If you've ever tried to invoke something that's not a function, you've probably seen an error message along the lines of `TypeError: undefined is not a function`. In this case, the property or variable doesn't exist at all. However, we'll get an error message along the same lines if we try to call an object that exists, but is not callable.

Sometimes this error is desirable, as our code is trying to call something that's not a function. The solution: we go and fix it. Remember that JavaScript is dynamically typed, and depending on how our application is designed, there could be circumstances where you need to explicitly check whether something is a function before trying to call it, as shown in the following example:

```
var object = {
    a: function() { return 'ret'; },
    b: []
};

_.isFunction(object.a) && object.a();
// → "ret"

_.isFunction(object.b) && object.b();
// → false
```

The first property, `a`, is a function, so the check issued by calling `isFunction()` passes, and the function is invoked. The `b` property, on the other hand, is an array and is not callable. So nothing happens there.

Assigning and accessing properties

Creating new JavaScript objects with values assigned to them is a straightforward task. The tedious part is when we have to merge the contents of one object into another or when we have to ensure that the default values are populated for the new objects. Locating values in objects and validating whether a key exists or not would actually require a significant amount of code were it not for the Lo-Dash tools that help us with these activities.

Extending objects

A common pattern in JavaScript libraries is to extend objects with other objects to assign property values. This can be done by assigning one property to an object on a statement-by-statement basis. The trouble with this approach is that you need to know ahead of time, exactly, which properties are going to be assigned to the destination object. Consider when new values come from a function argument. Having to know ahead of time all the possible properties these argument values might have isn't feasible. It's easier to just take what's passed as the source and extend the destination with it. That's why you'll find this pattern everywhere, including Lo-Dash. These tools are exposed for you to follow the same pattern in your application. An example for this is shown as follows:

```
var object = {
    name: 'Jeremy',
    age: 42
};

_.assign(object, {
    occupation: 'Programmer'
});

// →
// {
//   name: "Jeremy",
//   age: 42,
//   occupation: "Programmer"
// }
```

Here, the destination is the `object` variable and it gets the `occupation` property assigned to it. In fact, using `assign()`, we have to be careful because it pays no attention to the existing properties. Any sources passed in will override them, as shown in the following code:

```
var object1 = {
        name: 'Jenny',
        age: 27
    },
```

```
        object2 = {
            age: 31
        },
        object3 = {
            occupation: 'Neurologist'
        };

_.assign(object1, object2, object3);
// →
// {
//   name: "Jenny",
//   age": 31,
//   occupation: "Neurologist"
// }
```

Two objects are assigned to the destination, `object1`. The `assign()` function takes as many arguments as you need to pass—they're all chained together, from left to right, successively overriding the previous properties. In the preceding code, for example, there are no new objects being assigned that override the `name` property. The second object, though, overrides the `age` property. The final object has a brand new property and is simply added to the destination. Note that the final object is `object1`, which is modified in place.

> Lo-Dash uses aliases for some of its functions. For example, `extend()` is simply an alias for `assign()`; it does the exact same thing. It's a matter of personal taste, which one gets used. Do you prefer to think of an object being *assigned* to another or to think of one object *extending* another?

So far, we've dealt with simple properties that override one another, but what about more complex properties, such as objects and arrays? Would we like these values to merge together instead of being completely overridden? Here's an example showing this:

```
var object1 = {
        states: { running: 'poweroff' },
        names: [ 'CentOS', 'REHL' ]
    },
    object2 = {
        states: { off: 'poweron' },
        names: [ 'Ubuntu', 'Debian' ]
    };

_.merge(object1, object2, function(dest, src) {
    if (_.isArray(dest) && _.isArray(src)) {
```

```
            return dest.concat(src);
        }
    });
    // →
    // {
    //   states: {
    //     running: "poweroff",
    //     off: "poweron"
    //   },
    //   names: [
    //     "CentOS",
    //     "REHL",
    //     "Ubuntu",
    //     "Debian"
    //   ]
    // }
```

The `merge()` function will recursively examine the object's properties before overriding them, unlike the `assign()` function. In other respects, the two functions are similar, we're copying the properties of one or more objects to a single destination object. Notice the `states` property—it doesn't get overridden. Instead, `merge()` will examine the two objects and merge them together. Other types that already exist in the destination, with the same property name, are simply overridden. This includes arrays.

Notice that we're able to pass in your own callback function to `merge()`. This function determines how to merge properties. The code checks whether the destination property and the source property are arrays. If so, concatenate the source to the destination, otherwise it'll be overridden. The callback will ignore anything that's not an array.

Defaults for new objects

A common practice in JavaScript programming is to customize properties through arguments. That is, when we create a new object instance, we might supply an argument that's unique to the context where the object is being used. However, to use this pattern effectively, we have to provide some default values when the caller doesn't supply any values. There are a number of ways to do this, but Lo-Dash provides a function that will handle the vast majority of cases, as shown in the following code:

```
var object = {
    name: 'George'
};

_.defaults(object, {
```

```
        name: '',
        age: 0,
        occupation: ''
    });
    // →
    // {
    //   name: "George",
    //   age": 0,
    //   occupation": ""
    // }
```

As we can see, the `name` property isn't overridden with the default values. The other two defaults, `age` and `occupation`, are assigned to the object because they're undefined. If the property exists with any other value, `defaults()` will use that, and not the default.

> The `defaults()` function actually uses the `assign()` function. It just passes `assign()`, a callback function that customizes the way defaults are assigned. Namely, by looking for undefined values.

Finding keys and values

Objects, in Vanilla JavaScript, use the same syntax as arrays for accessing property values. That is, the square bracket notation but typically with a human-readable string, instead of a numerical index. However, the same issues that exist with numerical indices and arrays exist with objects and keys too. Just because the key is a string doesn't mean that we know which keys are available. Sometimes, we have to search the object to find the key we're looking for.

We use the `findKey()` function to locate the key of the first object property that callback returns truthy for:

```
var object = {
    name: 'Gene',
    age: 43,
    occupation: 'System Administrator'
};

_.findKey(object, function(value) {
```

```
    return value === 'Gene';
});
// → "name"
```

Here, the result is `name`; since it's the first property value our callback to `findKey()` returns `true` for. Strangely enough, the pluck style shorthand doesn't work the way you think it might. Calling `_.findKey(object, 'Gene')` doesn't find anything. That's because it's treating each of the property values as nested objects. Here's an example of how the where style shorthand works with this function:

```
var object = {
    programmers: {
        Keith: 'C',
        Marilyn: 'JavaScript'
    },
    designers: {
        Lori: 'CSS',
        Marilyn: 'HTML'
    }
};

_.findKey(object, { Marilyn: 'JavaScript' });
// → "programmers"
```

As we can see, it treats each property value as though it's another object; these are the values the `where` criteria is tested against. We can also find the key of object properties that have array values using the following code:

```
var object = {
    Maria: [
        'Python',
        'Lisp',
        'Go'
    ],
    Douglas: [
        'CSS',
        'Clojure',
        'Haskell'
    ]
};

var lang = 'Lisp';

_.findKey(object, function(value) {
```

```
        if (_.isArray(value)) {
            return _.contains(value, lang);
        } else {
            return value === lang;
        }
    });
    // → "Maria"
```

The callback function passed to `findKey()` checks whether the property value is an array. If so, it checks whether the value exists inside it. Otherwise, it'll just perform a strict value comparison. Since the `search` term exists in the first property value, the resulting key will be `Maria`.

> The `findKey()` function has a complementary function called `findLastKey()`. This simply searches in the opposite direction. It's kind of like `find()` and `findLast()` for collections. The difference is that the order is preserved in arrays. With objects, you're working with an unordered collection of key-value pairs. Since the order is never guaranteed, `findLastKey()` is limited in usefulness.

We might find ourselves working with an object, but we don't necessarily have a use for the keys. Remember that objects are also collections, so you can still use `find()` or `where()` as you would on arrays, as shown in the following example:

```
var object = {
    8490: {
        first: 'Arthur',
        last: 'Evans',
        enabled: false
    },
    7035: {
        first: 'Shirley',
        last: 'Rivera',
        enabled: false
    },
    4818: {
        first: 'William',
        last: 'Howard',
        enabled: true
    }
};

_.find(object, 'enabled');
// →
```

```
// {
//   first: "William",
//   last: "Howard",
//   enabled: true
// }

_.where(object, { last: 'Rivera' });
// →
// [
//   {
//     first: "Shirley",
//     last: "Rivera",
//     enabled: false
//   }
// ]
```

These functions treat each `object` property value as though they were an element of an array, ignoring the key. Next, we'll look at iterating through objects for cases when simple collection shorthands don't suffice.

Iterating over objects

Lo-Dash has a few functions that are useful when we need to iterate over the properties of an object in order to fulfill the behavior of our component. We'll start off by exploring some basic iterations. Then, we'll look at how to iterate over inherited object properties, followed by looking at keys and values and simple approaches to iterating over them.

Basic For Each

Just as we saw in the previous chapter, objects can be iterated, just as arrays—they're both collections. While the mechanism to do so is slightly different, Lo-Dash abstracts those differences away behind a unified function API, as shown in the following code:

```
var object = {
    name: 'Vince',
    age: 42,
    occupation: 'Architect'
}, result = [];

_.forOwn(object, function(value, key) {
    result.push(key + ': ' + value);
});
// →
```

```
// [
//    "name: Vince",
//    "age: 42",
//    "occupation: Architect"
// ]
```

The preceding code should look somewhat familiar. It's just like the `forEach()` function. Instead of the index, the second argument passed to the callback function is the property key.

> The `_.forOwn()` and `_.forEach()` functions behave identically when applied to an object. Both of these functions share the same base function that's used to iterate over collections. Lo-Dash has several base functions that are generic enough to serve many purposes. While these aren't exposed as a part of the public API, they make the exposed functions smaller and more comprehensible.

Including inherited properties

The object iterations only include *own* properties. That is, properties defined directly on the object and not elsewhere higher up in the **prototype chain**. We can test that the property in question is an owned property using the `hasOwnProperty()` method. We pass this method the name of the property we're looking for and it'll return `true` if the property is defined on this property and not further up in the prototype chain.

> If the term prototype chain sounds foreign, you might want to read about what they are and how they work. JavaScript objects are prototypical, so understanding this concept is important if you're a JavaScript programmer. This topic goes way beyond the scope of this book, but there are literally hundreds of excellent resources on prototypes available online. You don't need a full understanding of the topic for this book, just this section.

Lo-Dash has another object iteration function called `forIn()`. This function has the ability to iterate over both the owned properties, and over properties inherited through the prototype chain. An example for this is as follows:

```
function Person() {
    this.full = function() {
```

```
        return this.first + ' ' + this.last;
    };
}

function Employee(first, last, occupation) {
    this.first = first;
    this.last = last;
    this.occupation = occupation;
}

Employee.prototype = new Person();

var employee = new Employee('Theo', 'Cruz', 'Programmer'),
    resultOwn = [],
    resultIn = [];

_.forOwn(employee, function(value, key) {
    resultOwn.push(key);
});
// → [ "first", "last", "occupation" ]

_.forIn(employee, function(value, key) {
    resultIn.push(key);)
});
// → [ "first", "last", "occupation", "full" ]
```

This code uses both the forms of object iteration, `forOwn()`, followed by `forIn()`. The difference between the two is the `full` key, which only appears in the result generated by `forIn()`. That's because it's defined in the `Person` object, which is the prototype of `Employee`.

Keys and values

Previously, we've been working with Lo-Dash functions that directly iterate over the object's keys and values. This is the direct route. However, what if we've already written some code that's expecting an array of keys or values? There's an indirect route to iterating over objects that involves fetching the object's keys or its values as an array. You then iterate those.

For example, here's some code that will iterate over an object's keys:

```
var object = {
    occupation: 'Optometrist',
```

```
        last: 'Lynch',
        first: 'Shari'
};

_.sortBy(_.keys(object));
;
// → [ "first", "last", "occupation" ]
```

The preceding result is an array of strings built by the `keys()` function. We use the `sortBy()` function as a quick-and-dirty means to sort the array. Each property key is then pushed, in order, into the `result` array. Let's build this example and use it as a means to gain ordered access to object property values:

```
var object = {
        occupation: 'Optometrist',
        last: 'Lynch',
        first: 'Shari'
};

return _.at(object, _.sortBy(_.keys(object)));
// → [ "Shari", "Lynch", "Optometrist" ]
```

This code takes a bit of a shortcut. However, isn't that what writing good code is all about? Instead of employing the `forEach()` function to iterate the keys once they've been sorted, we simply pass them to the `at()` function. This function accepts an array of keys or indices and will look up the values for us, in order. The preceding result is an array of property values, sorted by their keys.

> The `keys()` function plays a vital role in the `forOwn()` function used to iterate over objects. This function is used to get the object keys, then the keys are iterated over, looking up object values. Again, some of the external Lo-Dash functions play an essential role internally.

Complementary to `keys()` is `values()` when you really have no use for key names. For example, to build an array of object values, you can use the following code:

```
var object = {
        first: 'Hue',
        last: 'Burton',
        occupation: 'Horticulturalist'
};

_.values(object);
// → [ "Hue", "Burton", "Horticulturalist" ]
```

From this point forward, we have an array of values to work with. The keys are disregarded completely. For instance, what if we wanted to sort the `object` property values by something specific to the value instead of a key, as we saw earlier? This can be done using the following code:

```
var object = {
    Angular: { name: 'Patrick' },
    Ember: { name: 'Jane' },
    Backbone: { name: 'George' }
};

_.sortBy(_.values(object), 'name');
// →
// [
//   { name: "George" },
//   { name: "Jane" },
//   { name: "Patrick" }
// ]
```

It's like we're just turning `object` into an array by truncating the keys. In fact, replacing `values()` with `toArray()` yields the exact same result. Under the hood, `toArray()` actually calls `values()` if an object is passed to it.

Calling methods

Objects don't just come with static property values—some of these values are callable functions. Functions assigned as an object's property are often referred to as methods, since they're generally interacting with the encapsulated state of the object to which they belong. Other times, objects are just a convenient vehicle for assigning and passing functions around the code. At the end of the day, they're just functions assigned to property values and Lo-Dash has some functions that assist with finding and calling them.

Getting results

We can use the `result()` function when we're unsure whether a given property name is a function or another type. This can simplify our code greatly because we don't need to write code that checks whether the property should be accessed like a regular static property value or if the property needs to be invoked. The usage of the `result()` function is shown in the following code:

```
var object1 = {
        name: 'Brian'
    },
```

```
    object2 = {
        name: function() {
            return 'Brian';
        }
    },
    object3 = {};

_.result(object1, 'name', 'Brian');
// → "Brian"

_.result(object2, 'name', 'Brian');
// → "Brian"

_.result(object3, 'name', 'Brian');
// → "Brian"
```

We can see that the result is always `Brian` and that the invocation of `result()` is the same on all the three objects. However, the result is `Brian` for three different reasons. The first object has a `name` property whose string value is `Brian`. The second object has a `name` property whose value is a function that returns the string `Brian`. The third object has no `name` attribute, so the default `Brian` value is used. With very little effort on your part, using the `result()` function's objects promotes consistency in terms of object property access.

Use `result()` judiciously, otherwise we'll get confused by its constant use in our code. In cases where direct property access or direct method invocation produces cleaner code, go that route. In cases where consistent results from property access presents a problem, and these should be rare, `result()` is our friend.

Finding methods

Before we call a method, we might want to execute some more complex logic than a simple default value if the method doesn't exist. For example, we might know that a `name()` method exists on some objects, but not on others. Something else we know for certain is that there's no `name` property with simple values, so the `result()` function doesn't help here.

The `functions()` function will look through an object and return an array of keys whose values are functions, as shown in the following code:

```
function Person(first, last) {
    this.first = first;
```

```
    this.last = last;
}

Person.prototype.name = function() {
    return this.first + ' ' + this.last;
};

_.functions(new Person('Teresa', 'Collins'));
// → [ "name" ]
```

Notice that the `name()` method is defined as a part of the person's prototype and not directly on the `Person` instance. This makes sense if we think about it. If the method exists higher up in the prototype chain, it's still callable, using the current instance as its context. So we would want those method names in the resulting array, and that's what happened here.

Transforming objects

Sometimes, we're implementing a feature and the given object we're working with just doesn't fit the bill—you need to transform it into a structure that's better suited for our needs. There are a handful of functions that are shipped with Lo-Dash to help us do this. We can create an array of arrays out of objects, we can pick and choose which object properties we want to work with, and we can turn an object inside out by inverting its keys and values.

Using pairs

The `pairs()` function accepts an object argument and generates an array of which each element is itself an array, which contains the key and the value. This structure can be a lot more convenient to work with under some circumstances. An example of this is shown in the following code:

```
function format(label, value) {
    return label + ': ' + value;
}
var object = {
    first: 'Katherine',
    last: 'Bailey',
    age: 33
}, result = '';

_.forEach(_.pairs(object), function(pair) {
```

```
        result += format.apply(null, pair) + '\n';
});
// → "first: Katherine\nlast: Bailey\nage: 33\n"
```

This code iterates over `object`, but before doing so, it calls the `pairs()` function. This transforms the object into an array, so the callback to `forEach()` gets an item of this array. The `pair` argument is an array, the first element is the key, and the second is the value. Using this key-value pair, we can call `apply()` on the `format()` function.

This means that if we have a generic callback function that's using something like the `format()` function, we don't need to pass it specific arguments. As it's illustrated here, when passing the `pair` array, you can call `apply()`.

Picking and omitting properties

Sometimes not every object property is necessary. In the case of extending an object with another, it can actually be a harmful exercise—adding properties that aren't needed. Instead, you can use the `pick()` function to choose the properties you need:

```
var object1 = {
        name: 'Kevin Moore',
        occupation: 'Programmer'
    },
    object2 = {
        specialty: 'Python',
        employer: 'Acme'
    };

_.assign(object1, _.pick(object2, 'specialty'));
// →
// {
//   name: "Kevin Moore",
//   occupation: "Programmer",
//   specialty: "Python"
// }
```

The second object in this example has only one property we're interested in, `specialty`. As it so happens, only one property is dropped, `employer`. However, what we've done here, by picking only what we need to extend our existing object with, is rule out the possibility of any unwanted properties causing issues down the line.

On the other hand, we might know exactly what we don't want from an object. The complementary to `pick()` is `omit()` that excludes the specified properties from the object, an example is shown here:

```
var object1 = {
        name: 'Kevin Moore',
        occupation: 'Programmer'
    },
    object2 = {
        specialty: 'Python',
        employer: 'Acme'
    };

_.assign(object1, _.omit(object2, 'employer'));
// →
// {
//   name: "Kevin Moore",
//   occupation: "Programmer",
//   specialty: "Python"
// }
```

This code is the inverse of the example on `pick()`. Instead of using `pick()` to specify what we want to have included, we use `omit()` to specify what we want excluded from the assignment. Which one we use depends on the requisite knowledge we have about the objects and which properties are valuable where.

Aside from providing the names of properties we want to be included or excluded, we can provide custom logic that makes the decision in the form of a callback using the following code:

```
var object = {
    name: 'Lois Long',
    age: 0,
    occupation: null
};

_.omit(object, function(value) {
    return !(!_.isBoolean(value) && value);
});
// → { name: "Lois Long" }
```

This code works in the same vein as `compact()` does with collections. Our callback is applied to every `object` property value, and if it returns `true`, then that value is omitted from the resulting object. Here, we're omitting falsey values with the exception of Boolean types.

Inverting keys and values

Our application might define a function that uses `keys()` or `values()` to work with an object. However, we might find ourselves in a situation where we want that same function to work inversely. That is, if the function uses `keys()`, we want it to use `values()`. If it uses `values()`, we want it to use `keys()`.

Rather than altering the function that's used everywhere and we know is stable, we can simply invert the object using Lo-Dash's `invert()` function before it's passed:

```
function sortValues(object) {
    return _.values(object).sort();
}

var object1 = {
        first: 'Mathew',
        last: 'Johnson'
    },
    object2 = {
        first: 'Melissa',
        last: 'Willians'
    };

sortValues(object1);
// → [ "Johnson", "Mathew" ]

sortValues(_.invert(object2));
// → [ "first", "last" ]
```

The `sortValues()` function is straightforward enough. It accepts an `object` argument, uses the `values()` function to build a property value array, then returns that array once it's been sorted. If we would like to reuse `sortValues()` on the object keys, for whatever reason, we just use `invert()` on the object before it's passed. This makes the keys of the object the values. So, when `sortValues()` calls the `values()` function, it's actually getting the keys.

Creating and cloning objects

Our last topic of the chapter is that of creating and cloning JavaScript objects. We can get by on a day-to-day basis without putting too much thought into creating or cloning objects. The `new` keyword or the object literal notation serves us just fine. Rarely is there a need to clone objects. However, Lo-Dash nonetheless has tools to deal with both of these scenarios when the need arises.

Creating objects

The `create()` function helps us close the gap between functional and object-oriented paradigms. It allows us to leverage some crucial functional JavaScript components in our objects. Particularly, when it comes to specifying prototypes when creating new objects.

This might not sound like a big deal, but it can make for some fun, elaborate hacking. Let's say that we have a collection of objects defined using the literal notation. These objects have just straightforward string property values. Let's also say that we have a class that defines some behavior through methods. Using the `create()` function, we can pass the property values directly to a new instance of that class, so that you can utilize its behavior, as shown in the following code:

```
function Person() {}
Person.prototype.name = function() {
    return this.first + ' ' + this.last;
};

var collection = [
        { first: 'Jean', last: 'Flores' },
        { first: 'Edward', last: 'Baker' },
        { first: 'Jennifer', last: 'Walker' }
    ],
    people = [];

_.forEach(collection, function(item) {
    people.push(_.create(Person.prototype, item));
});

_.invoke(people, 'name');
// → [ "Jean Flores", "Edward Baker", "Jennifer Walker" ]
```

It's helpful in the preceding example to think of the `Person` object as a contract or an interface. We then bind that contract to each object in the collection using the `create()` function. Now, each of these objects in the collection has a `name()` method, and we prove this by generating an array of names using the `invoke()` function that will invoke the given method name for each item in the collection.

Cloning objects

Creating the same object instance over and over again can lead to repetitive code. Especially, if we're using the object literal syntax. An alternative is to extend a new object with the new properties, but that can be problematic if we're trying to duplicate something that's not a plain object. Lo-Dash has a `clone()` function that's versatile enough to make a copy of just about anything, including deeply-nested objects. This versatility comes at a performance cost, so use it wisely. An example of using the `clone()` function is as follows:

```
function Person(first, last) {
    this.first = first;
    this.last = last;
}

var object1 = {
        first: 'Laura',
        last: 'Gray'
    },
    object2 = new Person('Bruce', 'Price'),
    clone1 = _.clone(object1),
    clone2 = _.clone(object2);

clone1.first === 'Laura';
// → true

clone2.first === 'Bruce' && clone2 instanceof Person;

// → false
```

The `object1` variable holds a plain object, while the `object2` variable holds an instance of the `Person` class, but they're essentially the same things. They both have `first` and `last` properties. The `clone1` and `clone2` variables hold their respective clones. What's interesting is the assertions we perform next. The first one passes because we're just verifying that the string in the original `name` property still exists in the cloned property. The second assertion fails, and not because the `first` property of the clone doesn't equal `Bruce`. It fails because `clone2` isn't an instance of `Person`. Instead, it's an instance of `Object` because the `clone()` function doesn't take the necessary steps of setting up the appropriate constructor property, and so on.

Other than the cloned object not being an instance of the `Person` class, it's pretty much the same object and attribute access, and so on. It should still work as it would on a plain object. The focus of `clone()` is really about duplicating a plain object so as to break the reference to the original. Then it can be manipulated without touching the source.

Summary

This chapter introduced us to how we can use Lo-Dash functions to perform sophisticated object interactions. We started with the utilities that made reasoning about the JavaScript type system a little less painful. Next, we saw how object properties can be accessed and assigned in various contexts. Iterating through object properties was the next topic, and there's an abundance of tools at your disposal in Lo-Dash here. In particular, iterating over only an object's keys or values would require a lot of boilerplate code, were it not for the Lo-Dash functions that take care of this for us. Transformations take place when we pass an object to a Lo-Dash function and it yields a new structure. Like when we're looking for a collection of key-value pairs. Picking or omitting properties is a really straightforward activity too. We wrapped up the chapter by taking a look at object creation and cloning facilities. These help us when we need to bend the rules a little to meet the needs of our application.

Through the first two chapters, you've probably noticed that there are a lot of functions being defined and used. That's no accident—JavaScript embraces the function as a first-class citizen, and Lo-Dash is no different. Functions are the focus of the next chapter.

3
Working with Functions

You'll find functions everywhere within a sufficiently large piece of JavaScript code. That's because they're treated in the same way as any other primitive type. Everything is an object in JavaScript, including functions. Functions have a context and a prototype, and they can be assigned to a new context and to variables.

Lo-Dash helps to best utilize functions. Where there are missing pieces, the utilities that Lo-Dash provides let us write some truly elegant, functional code. This chapter dives into these utilities. Whether we're changing the meaning of `this` or decorating an existing function, we'll walk through examples that illustrate how to get started.

In this chapter, we will cover the following topics:

- Binding function contexts
- Decorating functions
- Function constraints
- Timed execution
- Composing and currying functions

Binding function contexts

Every JavaScript function has a context. If you're coming from an object-oriented language, the function context is a lot like the object a method belongs to. The difference of course is that JavaScript doesn't classify objects in the object-oriented sense of the concept. Instead, functions are bound to a default context, and this can easily be changed at runtime. There are even built-in language mechanisms to make this happen.

Lo-Dash makes changing function contexts easy. We'll need to work with function contexts often when programming with Lo-Dash. We'll take a look at a number of approaches to working with and changing the context of functions now.

Changing the this keyword

Inside a function, the execution context is referred to by the `this` keyword. This is a special binding that we don't need to declare. It's always available to reference within a given function scope. It's important to keep in mind that it's entirely up to the caller, should he/she decide to override the meaning of `this`.

The `bind()` function is a powerful way to construct a new function that is permanently bound to the specified context. Here's a first look at how `bind()` works:

```
function sayWhat() {
    return 'Say, ' + this.what;
}

var sayHello = _.bind(sayWhat, {
    what: 'hello'
});

var sayGoodbye = _.bind(sayWhat, {
    what: 'goodbye'
});

sayHello();
// → "Say, hello"

sayGoodbye();
// → "Say, goodbye"
```

The preceding code defines a generic `sayWhat()` function that formats a string message based on the context for the function. In particular, it looks for the `what` property of the context. Next we use `bind()` to define two new functions based on `sayWhat()`. The `sayHello()` function is bound to a new context, while the `sayGoodbye()` function is bound to yet another context. The second argument to `bind()` is the object that becomes `this` in the function that's being bound. We can see that each of these contexts defines a unique `what` property value and this is reflected in the output of calling these two functions.

> Without Lo-Dash, we would rely on the `call()`, `apply()`, or `bind()` methods of the function to change its context. The advantage with the Lo-Dash `bind()` implementation is that it performs better because it's able to optimize better than the native methods.

The sayWhat() function didn't make use of any arguments. But just because we're fiddling with contexts doesn't mean the function we're binding can't accept arguments. Many functions make use of both arguments passed by the caller and the context object. Functions with custom contexts can indeed accept arguments. They can also be called with additional arguments after being bound to a new context, as shown in the following code:

```
function sayWhat(what) {
    if (_.isUndefined(what)) {
        what = this.what;
    }
    return 'Say, ' + what;
}

var sayHello = _.bind(sayWhat, {
    what: 'hello'
});

var sayGoodbye = _.bind(sayWhat, {}, 'goodbye'),
    saySomething = _.bind(sayWhat, {});

sayHello();
// → "Say, hello"

sayGoodbye();
// → "Say, goodbye"

saySomething('what?');
// → "Say, what?"
```

The sayWhat() function accepts a what parameter used to construct the string message. If this parameter is not supplied, it falls back to the what property of the context. Now we define three new functions, all with unique context and argument constraints. The sayHello() function isn't any different from the previous example; the what value is in the context. The sayGoodbye() function definition passes a third argument to bind(). After the context object, bind() will accept any number of arguments that are also bound to the function, but in a different way. This is called **partial application**, and we'll look at this later on in the chapter. The function is always bound, not only to the context, but to the argument values as well. Lastly, the saySomething() function is bound to a context that lacks the what property. Also, it is not bound to any what parameter. However, the what argument can still be supplied when the function is called, as is the case here.

Binding methods

There are no methods, per se, in JavaScript—just functions and context. However, that doesn't prevent programmers from following a more traditional object-oriented model.

If we assign a function to an object property, that object then becomes the context for the function. This is just the default behavior, and as the previous section illustrated, the context can change. However, the object to which the function belongs, being the default context, maps well to methods and encapsulation. The `bindAll()` function can help enforce this mapping:

```
function bindName(name) {
    return _.bind(name, {
        first: 'Becky',
        last: 'Rice'
    });
}

var object = {
    first: 'Ralph',
    last: 'Crawford',
    name: function() {
        return this.first + ' ' + this.last;
    }
};

var name = bindName(object.name);


object.name();
// → "Ralph Crawford"

name();
// → "Becky Rice"

_.bindAll(object);

name = bindName(object.name)

name();
// → "Ralph Crawford"
```

Let's walk through the bits of this experiment. The goal is to illustrate that once the `bindAll()` function is applied to an object, all methods belonging to that object have the context glued to it. It cannot change after this. First, the `bindName()` function just takes another function and binds it to the `Becky` context. We'll use this later on to prove a point.

The `object` variable holds a plain object with some simple properties and a simple method. The `name` variable is a function defined using the `bindName()` function. Notice that we're taking the `object.name()` method and assigning it a new context. The values we put in the `result` object confirm this. Next is the call to `bindAll()` on `object`. From this point onward, the `name()` method context can't change—it's glued to `object`. We then proceed to prove this fact by trying to bind it to a new context again, but `bindAll()` has enforced the context.

> When using `bindAll()`, you can unintentionally break other functionality in your application. The ability to change function context is a strength, not a weakness. Use `bindAll()` when you're absolutely certain that the method context should never change. If there's little to no chance of your method context changing when it shouldn't, don't bother with `bindAll()`.

The name `bindAll()` implies that this is an all or nothing operation, which actually isn't the case. We don't have to enforce the context of every method attached to your object. We can actually specify the method names as a second argument and only these methods are glued to the object context. This is illustrated in the following example:

```
function getName() {
    return this.name;
}

var object = {
    name: 'My Bound Object',
    method1: getName,
    method2: getName,
    method3: getName
};


_.bindAll(object, [ 'method1', 'method2' ]);

var method3 = _.bind(object.method3, {
```

```
        name: 'New Context'
    });

    object.method1();
    // → "My Bound Object"

    object.method2();
    // → "My Bound Object"

    method3();
    // → "New Context"
```

We can see that the call to `bindAll()` specifies that only `method1` and `method2` are bound to `object`. Later on, we actually try binding `method3` to a completely new context and it works as expected. Had we not limited the `bindAll()` call to specific methods, we wouldn't have been able to change the context of `method3`.

Dynamic methods

Methods can also lazily bind to objects. We can use the `bindKey()` function to construct a new function that will call the given method name on the given object. The method doesn't actually have to exist prior to calling `bindKey()`. That's the lazy part. And this comes in handy if you need to assign a method as a callback but aren't exactly sure if the method exists yet. Consider the following example:

```
function workLeft() {
    return 65 - this.age + ' years';
}

var object = {
    age: 38
};

var work = _.bindKey(object, 'work');

object.work = workLeft;

work();
// → "27 years"
```

Here we have an object with an `age` property. We also have a `workLeft()` function that computes a number based on the `age` property of the context. We could assign this function directly to the `work` property, but we've instead used the `bindKey()` function to construct a new function that will reference the `work()` method when called. The crucial thing to note is that we're able to build this callback function before the `work()` method exists in `object`. It gets added later. It could also get swapped out for a different implementation and would still call the appropriate method.

> The bound key has to exist when the function created by `bindKey()` is eventually called. Otherwise, you'll get a `TypeError`.

Just like a function that has been bound to a context using the `bind()` function, we still have freedom with the way arguments are managed. That is, we can bind argument values or supply argument values when the bound function is called, as shown in the following code:

```
function workLeft(retirement, period) {
    return retirement - this.age + ' ' + period;
}

var collection = [
    { age: 34, retirement: 60 },
    { age: 47 },
    { age: 28, retirement: 55 },
    { age: 41 }
];

var functions = [],
    result = [];

 _.forEach(collection, function(item) {
    functions.push(_.bindKey(item, 'work', item.retirement ?
        item.retirement : 65));
});

_.forEach(collection, function(item) {
```

```
        _.extend(item, { work: workLeft });
    });

    _.forEach(functions, function(item) {
        result.push(item('years'));
    });
    // →
    // [
    //   "26 years",
    //   "18 years",
    //   "27 years",
    //   "24 years"
    // ]
```

The `workLeft()` function depends on a couple of arguments and the `age` property of the context. Next, we define a collection of objects and a couple of empty arrays to perform our experiment. Now we have three `forEach()` iterations that demonstrate how arguments work with `bindKey()`.

The first iteration is over the collection and is where the `bindKey()` function is applied in order to generate a `work()` method. We can see that not every object in the collection has a `retirement` property value. If it doesn't, we bind `65` as the argument value. At this point, we have an array of functions, each bound to the `work()` method of their object. The second iteration populates the `work` property of each object in the collection, so now `work()` is a callable function.

The last iteration calls each of these bound method functions with another argument.

Decorating functions

A decorator does what the name implies. It decorates functions with additional capabilities. It's like an adornment for a piece of functionality. For example, let's say we've already implemented a function that looks up data in some structure. It's already used throughout our application, but now we're implementing a new component that requires this same functionality and something extra. We can use the function-decorating tools provided by Lo-Dash to take existing functions and extend them.

There are two flavors of Lo-Dash function decoration: **Partials**, which construct new functions that have the arguments of the original function partially supplied, and **Wrappers**, which build a new function that wraps the original function with a whole new function.

Partials

To create a partial function using Lo-Dash, you use the `partial()` function. The resulting function then has some arguments presupplied—we don't have to supply them again when called. This concept is really useful when we need to dynamically supply arguments to a function, just before it's passed to a new context where those arguments aren't available. This is also the case with callbacks, as shown in the following example:

```
function sayWhat(what) {
    return 'Say, ' + what;
}

var hello = _.partial(sayWhat, 'hello'),
    goodbye = _.partial(sayWhat, 'goodbye');

hello();
// → "Say, hello"

goodbye();
// → "Say, goodbye"
```

The `sayWhat()` function builds a simple string based on the supplied string argument. The two calls to `partial()` that follow supply this argument. The `hello()` and `goodbye()` functions, when called, will call `sayWhat()` with their respective partial arguments.

As we've seen so far in this chapter, many of the Lo-Dash functions that deal with functions return new ones. They also support the arguments passed by the caller. This is valuable because adding new parameters to our functions doesn't require changes to our function bindings, as shown here:

```
function greet(greeting, name) {
    return greeting + ', ' + name;
}

var hello = _.partial(greet, 'hello'),
    goodbye = _.partial(greet, 'goodbye');

hello('Fran');
// → "hello, Fran"

goodbye('Jacob');
// → "goodbye, Jacob"
```

The `greet()` function in the preceding code accepts two arguments, `greeting` and `name`. The `hello()` and the `goodbye()` functions are constructed as partial functions that call `greet()` with the first argument already supplied. Later on, when these functions are called, we can supply the more context-specific argument—`name`.

What if the context-specific argument were the first function argument? Can we still have the caller of the partial function supply the name? To answer this question, we turn to the `partialRight()` function:

```
function greet(name, greeting) {
    return greeting + ', ' + name;
}

var hello = _.partialRight(greet, 'hello'),
    goodbye = _.partialRight(greet, 'goodbye');

hello('Brent');
// → "hello, Brent"

goodbye('Alison');
// → "goodbye, Alison"
```

This code looks similar to the previous example, but there is one important difference. The `greet()` function expects the `name` parameter as the first argument. We want the caller to be able to specify this value, but we also want to specify `greeting` as a partial argument. The `partialRight()` function works the same as `partial()` except that it passes arguments to the function in a different order.

Partials aren't limited to our own functions. We can exploit this shorthand against Lo-Dash functionality itself. If you need to run a Lo-Dash function, in a callback for example, you can construct a new partial function that redefines the Lo-Dash function, with the arguments presupplied. This is shown in the following code:

```
var collection = [
    'Sheila',
    'Kurt',
    'Wade',
    'Kyle'
];

var random = _.partial(_.random, 1, collection.length),
    sample = _.partial(_.sample, collection);

random();
```

```
// → 4

sample();
// → "Wade"
```

Here we have a simple collection and two partial functions that operate on it. First, we utilize the `random()` Lo-Dash function, supplying the range as partial arguments. Then we utilize the `sample()` function, supplying the collection to sample as a partial argument.

Function decorators

We can utilize the `wrap()` function to decorate a value or another function with specific behavior. As with all other Lo-Dash function helpers, one advantage of using `wrap()` is that the caller of the generated function can supply more data via arguments, as demonstrated in the following code:

```
function strong(value) {
    return '<strong>' + value + '</strong>';
}

function regex(exp, val) {
    exp = _.isRegExp(exp) ?
        exp : new RegExp(exp);
    return _.isUndefined(val) ?
        exp : exp.exec(val);
}

var boldName = _.wrap('Marianne', strong),
    getNumber = _.wrap('(\\d+)', regex);

boldName();
// → "<strong>Marianne</strong>"

getNumber('abc123')[1];
// → "123"
```

The first function, `strong()`, wraps the value in `<strong/>` tags. The second function, `regex()`, is a little more involved. It wraps a value in a `RegExp` instance. But it's smart enough to do this only if the value is a string—if it's already a regular expression, there's no need to create another. Also, if a value is supplied to the second argument, it'll execute the regular expression against it, returning the result.

The result of calling `boldName()` is self-explanatory. The value `'Marianne'` is wrapped with the `strong()` function. The `getNumber()` function is a result of wrapping a regular expression string that looks for numbers. However, the call to `getNumber()` supplies an additional argument, that is, the call provides a string to execute the regular expression against it. This is why we access the result using a numerical index following the call.

Let's turn our attention to decorating existing functions with new functionality using `wrap()`:

```
var user = _.sample([
    'Scott',
    'Breanne'
]);

var allowed = [
    'Scott',
    'Estelle'
];

function permission(func) {
    if (_.contains(allowed, user)) {
        return func.apply(null, _.slice(arguments, 1));
    }
    throw new Error('DENIED');
}

function echo(value) {
    return value;
}

var welcome = _.wrap(echo, permission);

welcome('Yo there!');
```

The basic idea here is to decorate the `echo()` function with permission checking ability. The `permission()` function will call the function that is passed to it only if the `user` variable exists in the `allowed` array. An exception is raised if this is not the case. Repeatedly running this code will randomly generate denied errors. It all depends on whether `'Breanne'`, who isn't in the `allowed` array, is sampled as the current user or not.

Function constraints

Similar to decorating functions with new behavior are the constraints imposed on functions. This impacts when and how often the function can be called. Function constraints also control how values returned by calling a function are cached. Lo-Dash has functions that deal with each of these scenarios.

Limiting call counts

There are two Lo-Dash functions that deal with counting the number of times a given function is called. The `after()` function will execute a callback after the composed function is called a given number of times. The `once()` function constrains the given function to being called only once. Let's look at `after()` and see how it works:

```
function work(value) {
    progress();
}

function reportProgress() {
    console.log(++complete + '%');
    progress = complete < 100 ?
        _.after(0.01 * collection.length, reportProgress) :
        _.noop;
}

var complete = 0,
    collection = _.range(9999999),
    progress = _.noop;

reportProgress();

_.forEach(collection, work);
// →
// 1%
// 2%
// 3%
// …
```

The `work()` function is a contrived function that actually does nothing other than calling `progress()`, which notifies the world that progress has been made. A real function that actually did work would call `progress()` after having done the work. Next, we have a `reportProgress()` function. It is responsible for logging the progress. It also creates the `progress()` function using `after()`. Until the `complete` variable has reached 100 percent, it'll call `reportProgress()` again, which redefines the `progress()` function. The `after()` function will call the callback function supplied to it after the `progress()` function has been called `x` number of times. In this case, `x` is 1 percent of the collection length.

To sum up, `reportProgress()` defines the `progress()` function. This function is called by worker functions that need to notify the world about their progress. After `progress()` has been called so many times, `reportProgress()` is called. This is where the progress is logged and `progress()` is redefined.

All this is put into action by creating a rather large collection and iterating over it, calling `work()` along the way. But before the iterating starts, we kick off the progress tracker by calling `reportProgress()`. One nice aspect of this code is that there is a separation of concerns between tracking progress and performing work. The worker function only needs to worry about calling `progress()`. The `reportProgress()` is only concerned about periodically logging the progress and doesn't care about the actual work being done.

Asynchronous operations can make use of `after()` as well. The previous example explicitly called the function that was created by `after()`. However, what if we want to synchronize what happens after several asynchronous callback functions have fired? Let's find out using the following code:

```
function process(coll, callback) {
    var sync = _.after(coll.length, callback);
    _.forEach(coll, function() {
        setTimeout(sync, _.random(2000));
    });
    console.log('timeouts all set');
}

process(_.range(5), function() {
    console.log('callbacks completed');
});
// →
// timeouts all set
// callbacks completed
```

First, we have a `process()` function meant to symbolize a long-running asynchronous process—something that runs in the background, in other words. This function takes two arguments: a collection and a callback. The `callback` is a function that is called after each asynchronous operation on the collection has completed. We do this by creating a new `sync()` function using `after()`. The collection length is passed to `after()`. This means that after `sync()` has been called five times, which is the length of our collection, the callback is called.

Next, we randomly choose a timeout and call `sync()`—this is the asynchronous part. After all the timeouts have been set, we then log that the calls to `sync()` have been scheduled. The callback that executes when these are done logs a basic message.

Sometimes, it's useful to call a function just once. Beyond that, it is just useless repetition—harmless, but unnecessary. Therefore, a useful constraint for a function might be only allowing it to be called once. But how would we enforce such a thing? This can be done using the following code:

```
function getLeader(coll) {
    return _.first(_.sortBy(coll, 'score').reverse());
}

var collection = [
    { name: 'Dana', score: 84.4 },
    { name: 'Elsa', score: 44.3 },
    { name: 'Terrance', score: 55.9 },
    { name: 'Derrick', score: 86.1 }
];

var leader = _.once(getLeader);

leader(collection);
// → { name: "Derrick", score: 86.1 }
```

The `getLeader()` function in this code takes a collection and returns the name of the leader, according to the `score` property. We use this function to construct the `leader()` function. Using `once()`, we tell the `leader()` function to only call `getLeader()` once, and only once. You can't prevent the caller from making 50 calls to these functions. The job of the `once()` function is to encapsulate the function passed to it, storing the return value of the first invocation. If this value is set, it's cached for subsequent calls. So the preceding code assumes that the collection is unchanging and the leader will always be the same.

Caching values

The preceding example gave the first glimpse into caching values with Lo-Dash. If the function is constrained to be called only once, it might as well store the value of that first invocation. This is almost caching as a side effect—there's a more explicit approach that uses the `memoize()` function. Explicit caching is especially useful for mathematical functions, where given the same input, the same output is always produced. This is also referred to as **referential transparency**. An example for this is as follows:

```
function toCelsius(degrees) {
    return (degrees - 32) * 5 / 9;
}

function toFahrenheit(degrees) {
    return degrees * 9 / 5 + 32;
}

var celsius = _.memoize(toCelsius),
    fahrenheit = _.memoize(toFahrenheit);

toCelsius(89).toFixed(2) + ' C';
// → "31.67 C"

celsius(89).toFixed(2) + ' C';
// → "31.67 C"

toFahrenheit(23).toFixed(2) + ' F';
// → "73.40 F"

fahrenheit(23).toFixed(2) + ' F';
// → "73.40 F"
```

Here, we have two simple mathematical functions and they are good candidates for **memoization**. The `toCelsius()` function takes the given degrees in Fahrenheit and returns the Celsius equivalent. The `toFahrenheit()` function is the inverse—it takes a Celsius argument and returns a Fahrenheit value. We then take these two functions and wrap them with `memoize()`, yielding two new functions, `celsius()` and `fahrenheit()`.

After that, we make two calls each to the same function successively. The first call computes the value and stores it. The second call returns the cached result and computes nothing, but how does this cache lookup work? How does the memoized function know to use a value from the cache and not to compute a value? Let's find this out using the following code:

```
function toCelsius(degrees) {
    return (degrees - 32) * 5 / 9;
}

function toFahrenheit(degrees) {
    return degrees * 9 / 5 + 32;
}

function convertTemp(degrees, system) {
    return system.toUpperCase() === 'C' ?
        toFahrenheit(degrees).toFixed(2) + ' F' :
        toCelsius(degrees).toFixed(2) + ' C';
}

var convert = _.memoize(convertTemp, function(degrees, system) {
    return degrees + system;
});

convert(89, 'F');
convert(89, 'F');
convert(23, 'C');
convert(23, 'C');
```

By default, the resulting function generated by `memoize()` will use the first supplied argument as the cache key. The cache is a simple object and values are looked up by the property key. In the previous example, the memoized functions accepted only one argument. This is fine, but in more complex functions that accept more than one argument, you need a means to resolve the lookup key, as is illustrated in the preceding example.

This is basically a rewrite of the previous example, as it generates the same result. We still have the `toCelsius()` and `toFahrenheit()` functions, but we've introduced a new `convertTemp()` function. This function accepts two arguments: the `degrees` and the temperature `system` these degrees represent. Based on these argument values, we can make the appropriate call to either `toCelsius()` or `toFahrenheit()`.

We then construct the `convert()` function, a memoized version of `convertTemp()`. You'll notice the second function passed to `memoize()` here builds and returns a cache key. Without it, cache keys would still be consulted based only on the first argument value, which would return incorrect data. Be careful.

> You may have noticed that we could have continued using the previously cached functions, `celsius()` and `fahrenheit()`. That would mean a multilayered cache, which sounds kind of cool actually. Resist the temptation to do stuff like this. If you're performing badly enough to require a multilayer cache, it's time to reconsider the design at a higher level.

Timed execution

By nature, JavaScript code executes synchronously, that is, you don't have multiple threads of control, each running a piece of your code and competing for the CPU's attention. There are web workers in modern browsers, but these are far from commonplace yet and don't share much similarity with a threading API you'd find in another language. The upside to all of this is that you, as the programmer, don't need to concern yourself with synchronization primitives and all the other nasty details associated with multithreaded programming.

Instead, you face a different kind of difficulty in that you have to deal with events, the DOM, and other forms of callbacks; so much for synchronous code. Sometimes, this is actually desired. For example, you need to wait for a predetermined amount of time before something can happen. Or, perhaps you want to update the DOM and then pick up where you left off. Lo-Dash has tools that help you figure out the tricky details when it comes to timing function calls and coping with the side effects.

Delaying function calls

The `delay()` function is used to execute a given callback function after the given number of milliseconds has elapsed. This actually works the same way as the built-in `setTimeout()` function does. This is shown in the following code:

```
function poll() {
    if (++cnt < max) {
        console.log('polling round ' + (cnt + 1));
        timer = _.delay(poll, interval);
    } else {
```

```
        clearTimeout(timer);
    }
}

var cnt = -1,
    max = 5,
    interval = 3000,
    timer;

poll();
// →
// polling round 1
// polling round 2
// polling round 3
// polling round 4
// polling round 5
```

This code defines a `poll()` function that is used to periodically log which round of polling we're on. Polling is a common pattern used in frontends to synchronize data from the API, with what the user is looking at. We've set the `max` variable, which controls the number of polling iterations, to `5`. The `interval` variable is set to `3000` milliseconds. It controls the polling call frequency. You can see that the `poll()` function will first check whether we've already reached the maximum number of iterations or not. If not, the `timer` variable gets a timeout value—just an integer—by calling `delay()`. The `delay()` callback is `poll()`. If we've already reached our threshold, the timeout is cleared and there's no further poll scheduling.

If you look closely, you'll notice that there's no difference between using `delay()` and the built-in `setTimeout()` function. Both accept a callback function and duration as arguments, and both return a timeout number that can be cleared using `clearTimeout()`. What's interesting about `delay()` compared to `setTimeout()` is how they deal with arguments. Let's see how arguments are handled:

```
function sayHi(name, delay) {
    function sayHiImp(name) {
        console.log('Hi, ' + name);
    }
    if (_.isUndefined(delay)) {
        _.delay(sayHiImp, 1, name);
    } else {
        _.delay(sayHiImp, delay, name);
    }
}

sayHi('Jan');
```

```
sayHi('Jim', 3000);
// →
// Hi, Jan
// Hi, Jim
```

Here we've created a `sayHi()` function. This has a nested function within the called `sayHiImp()` function , which is the actual implementation. The `sayHi()` function is just a wrapper for `sayHiImp()`. It logs the given `name` parameter and checks whether the `delay` parameter was supplied or not; if not, it supplies a default `delay` value. It's important that our function either always runs synchronously or asynchronously, but never both. However, if there's a `delay` value, we use it with the `delay()` function to postpone the call to `sayHiImp()`. Notice that we pass the `name` parameter to the `delay()` call as well. Rather than having to construct our own partial function, we let `delay()` make one for us.

Deferring function calls

Whenever JavaScript code is run in the browser, it kicks off what is known as a **call stack**. Most programming languages share the notion of a call stack. It can be thought of as a traceable graph of function calls, starting with the root call. What's interesting is that the JavaScript call stack and the DOM are two completely separate entities that share the same thread of control. The implication is that the DOM doesn't run while there's an active JavaScript call stack. This is why long-running JavaScript code locks up UI interactivity.

Using the `defer()` function is a workaround for scenarios where you have a function that could take a while (a while being a relative term here—2 seconds is a while). You can push the call to that function till after the call stack has cleared, as shown in the following code:

```
function expensive() {
    _.forEach(_.range(Math.pow(2, 25)), _.noop);
    console.log('done');
}

_.defer(expensive);
console.log('computing...');
// →
// computing...
// done
```

The `expensive()` function does nothing but hog the CPU for a bit, preventing the `console.log()` call from running. So we use `defer()` to call `expensive()`, which waits till the current call stack has finished. The `'computing...'` string is logged as the last statement in the call stack. Shortly thereafter, the `'done'` string appears in the console log. The trick is that we're giving the DOM a chance to update before the expensive code runs.

An alternative approach to calling `defer()` every time you want to invoke something after the call stack has cleared is to create a wrapper function. You then call this wrapper as you would call any other function and it'll take care of deferring it for you. This is done using the following code:

```
function deferred(func) {
    return _.defer.apply(_, ([ func ])
        .concat(_.slice(arguments, 1)));
}

function setTitle(title) {
    console.log('Title: "' + title + '"');
}

function setState(app) {
    console.log('State: "' + app.state + '"');
}

var title = _.wrap(setTitle, deferred),
    state = _.wrap(setState, deferred),
    app = { state: 'stopped' };

title('Home');
state(app);
app.state = 'started';
// →
// Title: "Home"
// State: "started"
```

There are two functions here, `setTitle()` and `setState()`, both of which we'd like to be made deferrable. The first function takes a `title` argument and logs it. The second function takes an `app` object and logs the `state` property of that object. The `deferred()` function is a wrapper. We'll use it along with `wrap()` to make any function deferrable. All `deferred()` does is apply `defer()` to the function that was passed along with some arguments.

Next, you can see that the `title()` function is the deferred version of `setTitle()` while the `state()` function is the deferred version of `setState()`. We also have an `app` object with an initial state of `'stopped'`. Calling `title()` and `state()` will always be deferred to after the call stack clears. This point is further illustrated in the preceding code by setting the state to `started`, after the call to `state()`. You can guess which string is logged.

Throttling function calls

Often, events in the DOM can trigger much more frequently than you're equipped to handle them. The simple act of moving the mouse pointer around has the potential to generate hundreds of events per second. If each of these events has a handler and that handler does anything meaningful, the UI will lag. There's simply no way to keep up, no matter how fast the processor is. The only way to keep up is to ignore the majority of these events and only responds at a certain frequency. The idea is illustrated in the following code:

```
var el = document.querySelector('#container'),
    onMouseMove = _.throttle(function(e) {
        console.log('X: ' + e.clientX + ' Y: ' + e.clientY);
    }, 750);

el.addEventListener('mousemove', onMouseMove);
window.addEventListener('hashchange', function cleanup() {
    el.removeEventListener('mousemove', onMouseMove);
    window.removeEventListener('mousemove', cleanup);
});
```

The `el` variable is a DOM element that we want to listen to for `mousemove` events. The `onMouseMove` function is created by passing a function to `throttle()`. This callback simply logs the mouse coordinates. We also pass `750` to `throttle()` as the maximum frequency with this callback is allowed to run. Next, we bind the event and set up the cleanup actions to remove the listener when we're done with it. Had we not throttled `onMouseMove()`, you would see a noticeable difference in the `console.log()` verbosity.

Debouncing function calls

Debouncing functions is similar to throttling them. The difference is in what happens when the wait duration has elapsed. With `throttle()`, the function is invariably called. For example, if the `wait` value was set to `10` milliseconds on a throttled function, and the function was called during those 10 milliseconds, it'll get called before the next wait. With `debounce()`, during the 10-millisecond wait, if the function was called, it'll wait an additional 10 milliseconds. Let's look at some debouncing code:

```
function log(msg, item) {
    console.log(msg + ' ' + item);
}

var debounced = _.debounce(_.partial(log, 'debounced'), 1),
    throttled = _.throttle(_.partial(log, 'throttled'), 1),
    size = 1500;

_.forEach(_.range(size), debounced);
_.forEach(_.range(size), throttled);
```

We have a simple `log()` function that logs a message and an item number. We then proceed to build a `debounced()` and a `throttled()` version of the function. Then we run both through the same-sized loop. What's the difference? The output looks something like this:

```
throttled 0
throttled 1
throttled 744
debounced 1499
throttled 1499
```

What happened here? We set the `wait` time to `1` millisecond for both `debounced()` and `throttled()`. In the time it took to process `1500` items, the wait period elapsed twice for the `throttled()` function. As soon as that happened, the `log()` function was called, hence the output. Notice that the `debounce()` output happened only after the processing was done. That's because `debounce()` was called many times during the 1-millisecond wait, and again during the next wait.

> The `throttle()` function actually uses `debounce()` under the hood. All of the complexity is in `debounce()` and it accepts several configuration options. Among these are the **leading** and **trailing** edges of execution. What does this mean? You'll notice in the preceding output that the `throttled()` function is called after `debounce()`. That's the trailing edge of the wait period. The leading edge of the wait period is before the wait period starts. Both of these edges default to `true` for `throttle()`. This means that you're in an intense loop where your throttled function is being hammered, the function is called immediately, before waiting for the next call. Then, if the loop ends abruptly, the function is called again when the wait period ends.

Composing and currying functions

The last section of this chapter is about assembling functions that realize larger behavior out of smaller functions. There are two ways to assemble such functions. The first is to use the appropriately named `compose()` function, which performs a nested invocation of the provided functions, or where order is important, we can use the `flow()` function to return values together. Currying lets you adapt your function to be called successively in different contexts. Each of these Lo-Dash tools lets you take the existing functionality in your application and build on it in interesting ways.

Composing functions

The `compose()` function builds a new function out of the provided functions. When we call this new function, a nested invocation of the supplied function starts, that is, the last supplied function is called with any additional arguments. The returned value is then fed to the next function and so on, ultimately producing a value for the caller. This is better explained in the following example:

```
function dough(pizza) {
    if (_.isUndefined(pizza)) {
        pizza = {};
    }
    return _.extend({
        dough: true
    }, pizza);
}

function sauce(pizza) {
    if (!pizza.dough) {
```

```
        throw new Error('Dough not ready');
    }
    return _.extend({
        sauce: true
    }, pizza);
}

function cheese(pizza) {
    if (!pizza.sauce) {
        throw new Error('Sauce not ready');
    }
    return _.extend({
        cheese: true
    }, pizza);
}

var pizza = _.compose(cheese, sauce, dough);

pizza();
// → { cheese: true, sauce: true, dough: true }
```

There are three functions responsible for assembling pizza—`dough()`, `sauce()`, and `cheese()`. The job of each one of these functions is to set their corresponding attribute to `true` on the supplied `pizza` object. The `pizza()` function is composed using these functions which in turn use the `compose()` function. So calling `pizza()` will call `cheese(sauce(dough()))`. Note some of the checking that happens in these functions. For example, `dough()` will accept an object or construct a new one. However, the `sauce()` function won't work if there's no `dough` attribute. Likewise, `cheese()` complains if there's no `sauce`.

> While being able to compose functions is handy, it's a good idea to have precondition checking. Then they fail fast, so other developers attempting to compose something out of your functions have an obvious indication if something isn't possible.

If the reverse order of the function invocation is confusing, don't worry. We can reverse the order using the `flow()` function. Using the same `pizza` functions, we could make a slight modification to the `pizza()` composition function:

```
var pizza = _.flow(dough, sauce, cheese);

return pizza();
```

> The `compose()` function is actually an alias for the `flowRight()` function. The `flow()` and `flowRight()` functions are newer. In previous versions of Lo-Dash, the `compose()` function was standalone.

Currying functions

Have you ever found yourself having to create a bunch of variables that do nothing aside from eventually getting passed to a function? Instead of variable creation, the currying technique lets you partially apply the function. That is, you call the function, supplying only the data you have at that moment. Curried functions will keep returning the function until it has all the arguments necessary. This technique is explained using the following example:

```
function makePizza(dough, sauce, cheese) {
    return {
        dough: dough,
        sauce: sauce,
        cheese: cheese
    };
}

function dough(pizza) {
    return pizza(true);
}

function sauceAndCheese(pizza) {
    return pizza(true, true);
}

var pizza = _.curry(makePizza);

sauceAndCheese(dough(pizza));
// → { cheese: true, sauce: true, dough: true }
```

The `makePizza()` function has any arity of three—the number of arguments expected by the function. This means that the `pizza()` function created by calling `curry()` on `makePizza()` will keep returning the function until it's invoked with three arguments. We have the flexibility to pass these arguments however we want. This could be all three at once or it could be one at a time. This means that different contexts could pass data into the function, without the need to store them elsewhere.

Summary

Hopefully after reading this chapter, your appreciation for functions in JavaScript went up a little. Lo-Dash just makes functional programming in the frontend that much better. Functions in JavaScript are flexible by default, changing the execution context for example. This chapter showed you how some Lo-Dash functions make working with function contexts much easier by removing much of the boiler-plate code that would otherwise be needed. Partials are fundamental to functional programming, but it's one of those tasks that's anything but easy in JavaScript. Lo-Dash makes it easy to create partials and to decorate functions by wrapping them with additional logic.

We looked at functions that help constrain when a function should run. For example, should a function be allowed to run only once? Should the return values be cached? Timing the execution of functions is a complex topic, especially when you consider the DOM and how it integrates with the JavaScript call stack. Lo-Dash has a number of functions that deal with managing the timed execution of functions. We looked at these in detail.

The chapter wrapped up with a look at how to compose larger pieces of functionality out of smaller functions. Currying functions let you define functions flexible enough to be invoked in a number of contexts, reducing the need to temporarily store arguments before they're passed. And on that note, we covered the Lo-Dash fundamentals. The concepts you've learned so far about collections, objects, and functions are applicable throughout the remainder of the book. We're now ready to move on to mapping and reducing values, a powerful technique that you'll utilize over and over again when programming with Lo-Dash.

4

Transformations Using Map/Reduce

The preceding three chapters alluded to transformation possibilities with Lo-Dash. Whether you're working with collections, objects, or functions, a common pattern with Lo-Dash functions is transformation of the input by generating a new, albeit slightly altered, version. The idea of transforming values is central to applicative programming, where much of the code you write is a series of transformations. Beginning with this chapter, we're going to shift gears and look at transformations in more detail.

Particularly, we'll be looking at all the interesting things we can do with Lo-Dash and the map/reduce programming model. We'll start off with the basics, getting our feet wet with some basic mappings and basic reductions. As we progress through the chapter, we'll start introducing more advanced techniques to think about in terms of map/reduce with Lo-Dash.

The goal, once you've reached the end of this chapter, is to have a solid understanding of the Lo-Dash functions available that aid in mapping and reducing collections. Additionally, you'll start to notice how disparate Lo-Dash functions work together in the map/reduce domain. Ready?

In this chapter, we will cover the following topics:

- Plucking values
- Mapping collections
- Mapping objects
- Reducing collections
- Reducing objects
- Binding contexts
- Map/reduce patterns

Plucking values

We've already seen how values can be plucked from collections using the `pluck()` function in *Chapter 1, Working with Arrays and Collections*. Consider that your informal introduction to mapping, because that's essentially what it's doing. It's taking an input collection and mapping it to a new collection, plucking only the properties we're interested in. This is shown in the following example:

```
var collection = [
    { name: 'Virginia', age: 45 },
    { name: 'Debra', age: 34 },
    { name: 'Jerry', age: 55 },
    { name: 'Earl', age: 29 }
];

_.pluck(collection, 'age');
// → [ 45, 34, 55, 29 ]
```

This is about as simple a mapping operation as you'll find. In fact, you can do the same thing with `map()`:

```
var collection = [
    { name: 'Michele', age: 58 },
    { name: 'Lynda', age: 23 },
    { name: 'William', age: 35 },
    { name: 'Thomas', age: 41 }
];

_.map(collection, 'name');
// →
// [
//    "Michele",
//    "Lynda",
//    "William",
//    "Thomas"
// ]
```

As you'd expect, the output here is exactly the same as it would be with `pluck()`. In fact, `pluck()` is actually using the `map()` function under the hood. The callback passed to `map()` is constructed using `property()`, which just returns the specified property value. The `map()` function falls back to this plucking behavior when passed a string instead of a function.

With that brief introduction to the nature of mapping, let's dig a little deeper and see what's possible in mapping collections.

Mapping collections

In this section, we'll explore mapping collections. Mapping one collection to another ranges from composing simple—as we saw in the preceding section—to sophisticated callbacks. Callbacks that map each item in the collection can include or exclude properties and can calculate new values. We'll also address the issue of filtering collections and how this can be done in conjunction with mapping.

Including and excluding properties

When applied to an object, the `pick()` function generates a new object containing only the specified properties. The opposite function, `omit()`, generates an object with every property except those specified. Since these functions work fine for individual object instances, why not use them with a collection? You can use both of these functions to shed properties from collections by mapping them to new ones, as shown in the following code:

```
var collection = [
    { first: 'Ryan', last: 'Coleman', age: 23 },
    { first: 'Ann', last: 'Sutton', age: 31 },
    { first: 'Van', last: 'Holloway', age: 44 },
    { first: 'Francis', last: 'Higgins', age: 38 }
];

_.map(collection, function(item) {
    return _.pick(item, [ 'first', 'last' ]);
});
// →
// [
//   { first: "Ryan", last: "Coleman" },
//   { first: "Ann", last: "Sutton" },
//   { first: "Van", last: "Holloway" },
//   { first: "Francis", last: "Higgins" }
// ]
```

Here, we're creating a new collection using the `map()` function. The callback function supplied to `map()` is applied to each item in the collection. The `item` argument is the original item from the collection. The callback is expected to return the mapped version of that item and this version could be anything, including the original item itself.

> Be careful when manipulating the original item in `map()` callbacks. If the item is an object and it's referenced elsewhere in your application, it could have unintended consequences.

We're returning a new object as the mapped item in the preceding code. This is done using the `pick()` function. We only care about the `first` and the `last` properties. Our newly mapped collection looks identical to the original, except that no item has an `age` property. This newly-mapped collection is seen in the following code:

```
var collection = [
    { first: 'Clinton', last: 'Park', age: 19 },
    { first: 'Dana', last: 'Hines', age: 36 },
    { first: 'Pete', last: 'Ross', age: 31 },
    { first: 'Annie', last: 'Cross', age: 48 }
];

_.map(collection, function(item) {
    return _.omit(item, 'first');
});
// →
// [
//   { last: "Park", age: 19 },
//   { last: "Hines", age: 36 },
//   { last: "Ross", age: 31 },
//   { last: "Cross", age: 48 }
// ]
```

This code follows the exact same approach as the previous `pick()` code. The only difference is that we're excluding the `first` property from the newly-created collection. You'll also notice that we're passing a string containing a single property name instead of an array of property names.

In addition to passing strings or arrays as the argument to `pick()` or `omit()`, we can pass in a function callback. This is suitable when it's not very clear which objects in a collection should have which properties. Using a callback like this inside a `map()` callback lets us perform detailed comparisons and transformations on collections with very little code:

```
function invalidAge(value, key) {
    return key === 'age' && value < 40;
}

var collection = [
    { first: 'Kim', last: 'Lawson', age: 40 },
    { first: 'Marcia', last: 'Butler', age: 31 },
    { first: 'Shawna', last: 'Hamilton', age: 39 },
```

```
    { first: 'Leon', last: 'Johnston', age: 67 }
];

_.map(collection, function(item) {
    return _.omit(item, invalidAge);
});
// →
// [
//   { first: "Kim", last: "Lawson", age: 40 },
//   { first: "Marcia", last: "Butler" },
//   { first: "Shawna", last: "Hamilton" },
//   { first: "Leon", last: "Johnston", age: 67 }
// ]
```

The new collection generated by this code excludes the `age` property for items where the `age` value is less than `40`. The callback supplied to `omit()` is applied to each key-value pair in the object. This code is a good illustration of the conciseness achievable with Lo-Dash. There's a lot of iterative code running here, and there is no `for` or `while` statement in sight.

Performing calculations

It's time now to turn our attention to performing calculations in our `map()` callbacks. This entails looking at the item and, based on its current state, computing a new value that will be ultimately mapped to the new collection. This could mean extending the original item's properties or replacing one with a newly computed value. Whichever the case, it's a lot easier to map these computations than to write your own logic that applies these functions to every item in your collection. This is explained using the following example:

```
var collection = [
    { name: 'Valerie', jqueryYears: 4, cssYears: 3 },
    { name: 'Alonzo', jqueryYears: 1, cssYears: 5 },
    { name: 'Claire', jqueryYears: 3, cssYears: 1 },
    { name: 'Duane', jqueryYears: 2, cssYears: 0 }
];

_.map(collection, function(item) {
    return _.extend({
        experience: item.jqueryYears + item.cssYears,
        specialty: item.jqueryYears >= item.cssYears ?
            'jQuery' : 'CSS'
```

```
        }, item);
    });
    // →
    // [
    //   {
    //     experience": 7,
    //     specialty": "jQuery",
    //     name": "Valerie",
    //     jqueryYears": 4,
    //     cssYears: 3
    //   },
    //   {
    //     experience: 6,
    //     specialty: "CSS",
    //     name: "Alonzo",
    //     jqueryYears: 1,
    //     cssYears: 5
    //   },
    //   {
    //     experience: 4,
    //     specialty: "jQuery",
    //     name: "Claire",
    //     jqueryYears: 3,
    //     cssYears: 1
    //   },
    //   {
    //     experience: 2,
    //     specialty: "jQuery",
    //     name: "Duane",
    //     jqueryYears: 2,
    //     cssYears: 0
    //   }
    // ]
```

Here, we're mapping each item in the original collection to an extended version of it. Particularly, we're computing two new values for each item—`experience` and `specialty`. The `experience` property is simply the sum of the `jqueryYears` and `cssYears` properties. The `specialty` property is computed based on the larger value of the `jqueryYears` and `cssYears` properties.

Earlier, I mentioned the need to be careful when modifying items in `map()` callbacks. In general, it's a bad idea. It's helpful to try and remember that `map()` is used to generate new collections, not to modify existing collections. Here's an illustration of the horrific consequences of not being careful:

```
var app = {},
    collection = [
        { name: 'Cameron', supervisor: false },
        { name: 'Lindsey', supervisor: true },
        { name: 'Kenneth', supervisor: false },
        { name: 'Caroline', supervisor: true }
    ];

app.supervisor = _.find(collection, { supervisor: true });

_.map(collection, function(item) {
    return _.extend(item, { supervisor: false });
});

console.log(app.supervisor);
// → { name: "Lindsey", supervisor: false }
```

The destructive nature of this callback is not obvious at all and next to impossible for programmers to track down and diagnose. It is essentially resetting the `supervisor` property for each item. If these items are used anywhere else in the application, the `supervisor` property value will be clobbered whenever this map job is executed. If you need to reset values like this, ensure that the change is mapped to the new value and not made to the original.

Mapping also works with primitive values as the item. Often, we'll have an array of primitive values that we'd like transformed into an alternative representation. For example, let's say you have an array of sizes, expressed in bytes. You can map those arrays to a new collection with those sizes expressed as human-readable values, using the following code:

```
function bytes(b) {
    var units = [ 'B', 'K', 'M', 'G', 'T', 'P' ],
        target = 0;
    while (b >= 1024) {
        b = b / 1024;
        target++;
    }
    return (b % 1 === 0 ? b : b.toFixed(1)) +
        units[target] + (target === 0 ? '' : 'B');
}

var collection = [
    1024,
    1048576,
```

```
        345198,
        120120120
    ];

    _.map(collection, bytes);
    // → [ "1KB", "1MB", "337.1KB", "114.6MB" ]
```

The `bytes()` function takes a numerical argument, which is the number of bytes to be formatted. This is the starting unit. We just keep incrementing the `target` unit until we have something that is less than `1024`. For example, the last item in our collection maps to `'114.6MB'`. The `bytes()` function can be passed directly to `map()` since it's expecting values in our collection as they are.

Calling functions

We don't always have to write our own callback functions for `map()`. Wherever it makes sense, we're free to leverage Lo-Dash functions to map our collection items. For example, let's say we have a collection and we'd like to know the size of each item. There's a `size()` Lo-Dash function we can use as our `map()` callback, as follows:

```
var collection = [
    [ 1, 2 ],
    [ 1, 2, 3 ],
    { first: 1, second: 2 },
    { first: 1, second: 2, third: 3 }
];

_.map(collection, _.size);
// → [ 2, 3, 2, 3 ]
```

This code has the added benefit that the `size()` function returns consistent results, no matter what kind of argument is passed to it. In fact, any function that takes a single argument and returns a new value based on that argument is a valid candidate for a `map()` callback. For instance, we could also map the minimum and maximum value of each item:

```
var source = _.range(1000),
    collection = [
        _.sample(source, 50),
        _.sample(source, 100),
        _.sample(source, 150)
    ];

_.map(collection, _.min);
```

```
// → [ 20, 21, 1 ]

_.map(collection, _.max);
// → [ 931, 985, 991 ]
```

What if we want to map each item of our collection to a sorted version? Since we do not sort the collection itself, we don't care about the item positions within the collection, but the items themselves, if they're arrays, for instance. Let's see what happens with the following code:

```
var collection = [
    [ 'Evan', 'Veronica', 'Dana' ],
    [ 'Lila', 'Ronald', 'Dwayne' ],
    [ 'Ivan', 'Alfred', 'Doug' ],
    [ 'Penny', 'Lynne', 'Andy' ]
];

_.map(collection, _.compose(_.first, function(item) {
    return _.sortBy(item);
}));

// → [ "Dana", "Dwayne", "Alfred", "Andy" ]
```

This code uses the `compose()` function to construct a `map()` callback. The first function returns the sorted version of the item by passing it to `sortBy()`. The `first()` item of this sorted list is then returned as the mapped item. The end result is a new collection containing the alphabetically-first item from each array in our collection, with three lines of code. Not bad.

Filtering and mapping

Filtering and mapping are two closely related collection operations. Filtering extracts only those collection items that are of particular interest. Mapping transforms collections to produce new collections. But what if we only want to map a certain subset of our collection? Then it would make sense to chain together the filtering and mapping operations, right? Here's an example of what that might look like:

```
var collection = [
    { name: 'Karl', enabled: true },
    { name: 'Sophie', enabled: true },
    { name: 'Jerald', enabled: false },
```

```
        { name: 'Angie', enabled: false }
    ];

    _.compose(
        _.partialRight(_.map, 'name'),
        _.partialRight(_.filter, 'enabled')
    )(collection);
    // → [ "Karl", "Sophie" ]
```

This map is executed using `compose()` to build a function that is called right away, with our `collection` as the argument. The function is composed of two partials. We're using `partialRight()` on both arguments because we want the collection supplied as the leftmost argument in both cases. The first partial function is `filter()`. We're partially applying the `enabled` argument. So this function will filter our collection before it's passed to `map()`. The result of filtering the collection is passed to `map()`, which has the `name` argument partially applied. The end result is a collection with enabled `name` strings.

> The important thing to note about the preceding code is that the filtering operation takes place *before* the `map()` function is run. We could have stored the filtered collection in an intermediate variable instead of streamlining with `compose()`. Regardless of flavor, it's important that the items in your mapped collection correspond to the items in the source collection. It's conceivable to filter out the items in the `map()` callback by not returning anything, but this is ill-advised as it doesn't map well, both figuratively and literally.

Mapping objects

The previous section focused on collections and how to map them. But wait, objects are collections too, right? That is indeed correct, but it's worth differentiating between arrays and plain objects. The main reason is that there are implications with ordering and keys when performing map/reduce. At the end of the day, arrays and objects serve different use cases with map/reduce, and this chapter tries to acknowledge these differences.

Now we'll start looking at some techniques Lo-Dash programmers employ when working with objects and mapping them to collections. There are a number of factors to consider, such as the keys within an object, and calling methods on objects. We'll take a look at the relationship between key-value pairs and how they can be used in a mapping context.

Working with keys

We can use the keys of a given object in interesting ways to map the object to a new collection. For example, we can use the `keys()` function to extract the keys of an object and map them to values other than the property value, as shown in the following example:

```
var object = {
    first: 'Ronald',
    last: 'Walters',
    employer: 'Packt'
};

_.map(_.sortBy(_.keys(object)), function(item) {
    return object[item];
});
// → [ "Packt", "Ronald", "Walters" ]
```

The preceding code builds an array of property values from `object`. It does this using `map()`, which is actually mapping the `keys()` array of `object`. These keys are sorted using `sortBy()`. So `Packt` is the first element of the resulting array because `employer` is alphabetically-first in the `object` keys.

Sometimes, it's desirable to perform lookups in other objects and map those values to a target object. For example, not all APIs return everything you need for a given page, packaged in a neat little object. You have to do joins and build the data you need. This is shown in the following code:

```
var users = {},
    preferences = {};

_.each(_.range(100), function() {
    var id = _.uniqueId('user-');
    users[id] = { type: 'user' };
    preferences[id] = { emailme: !!(_.random()) };
});

_.map(users, function(value, key) {
    return _.extend({ id: key }, preferences[key]);
});
// →
// [
//   { id: "user-1", emailme: true },
//   { id: "user-2", emailme: false },
//   ...
// ]
```

This example builds two objects, `users` and `preferences`. In the case of each object, the keys are user identifiers that we're generating with `uniqueId()`. The `user` objects just have some dummy attribute in them, while the `preferences` objects have an `emailme` attribute, set to a random Boolean value.

Now let's say we need quick access to this preference for all users in the `users` object. As you can see, it's straightforward to implement using `map()` on the `users` object. The callback function returns a new object with the user ID. We extend this object with the preference for that particular user by looking them up by `key`.

Calling methods

Object properties aren't limited to storing primitive strings and numbers. Properties can store functions as their values, or methods, as they're commonly referred. However, depending on the context where you're using your object, methods aren't always callable, especially if you have little or no control over the context where your objects are used. One technique that's helpful in situations such as these is mapping the result of calling these methods and using this result in the context in question. Let's see how this can be done with the following code:

```
var object = {
    first: 'Roxanne',
    last: 'Elliot',
    name: function() {
        return this.first + ' ' + this.last;
    },
    age: 38,
    retirement: 65,
    working: function() {
        return this.retirement - this.age;
    }
};

_.map(object, function(value, key) {
    var item = {};
    item[key] = _.isFunction(value) ? object[key]() : value
    return item;
});
// →
// [
//   { first: "Roxanne" },
//   { last: "Elliot" },
```

```
//    { name: "Roxanne Elliot" },
//    { age: 38 },
//    { retirement: 65 },
//    { working: 27 }
// ]

_.map(object, function(value, key) {
    var item = {};
    item[key] = _.result(object, key);
    return item;
});
// →
// [
//    { first: "Roxanne" },
//    { last: "Elliot" },
//    { name: "Roxanne Elliot" },
//    { age: 38 },
//    { retirement: 65 },
//    { working: 27 }
// ]
```

Here, we have an object with both primitive property values and methods that use these properties. Now we'd like to map the results of calling those methods and we will experiment with two different approaches. The first approach uses the `isFunction()` function to determine whether the property value is callable or not. If it is, we call it and return that value. The second approach is a little easier to implement and achieves the same outcome. The `result()` function is applied to the object using the current key. This tests whether we're working with a function or not, so our code doesn't have to.

> In the first approach to mapping method invocations, you might have noticed that we're calling the method using `object[key]()` instead of `value()`. The former retains the context as the object variable, but the latter loses the context, since it is invoked as a plain function without any object. So when you're writing mapping callbacks that call methods and not getting the expected results, make sure the method's context is intact.

Perhaps you have an object but you're not sure which properties are methods. You can use `functions()` to figure this out and then map the results of calling each method to an array, as shown in the following code:

```
var object = {
    firstName: 'Fredrick',
```

```
    lastName: 'Townsend',
    first: function() {
        return this.firstName;
    },
    last: function() {
        return this.lastName;
    }
};

var methods = _.map(_.functions(object), function(item) {
    return [ _.bindKey(object, item) ];
});

_.invoke(methods, 0);
// → [ "Fredrick", "Townsend" ]
```

The `object` variable has two methods, `first()` and `last()`. Assuming we didn't know about these methods, we can find them using `functions()`. Here, we're building a `methods` array using `map()`. The input is an array containing the names of all the methods of the given object. The value we're returning is interesting. It's a single-value array; you'll see why in a moment. The value of this array is a function built by passing the object and the name of the method to `bindKey()`. This function, when invoked, will always use `object` as its context.

Lastly, we use `invoke()` to invoke each method in our `methods` array, building a new result array. Recall that our `map()` callback returned an array. This was a simple hack to make `invoke()` work, since it's a convenient way to call methods. It generally expects a key as the second argument, but a numerical index works just as well, since they're both looked up the same.

Mapping key-value pairs

Just because you're working with an object doesn't mean it's ideal, or even necessary. That's what `map()` is for—mapping what you're given to what you need. For instance, the property values are sometimes all that matter for what you're doing, and you can dispense with the keys entirely. For that, we have the `values()` function and we feed the values to `map()`:

```
var object = {
    first: 'Lindsay',
    last: 'Castillo',
```

```
    age: 51
};

_.map(_.filter(_.values(object), _.isString), function(item) {
    return '<strong>' + item + '</strong>';
});
// → [ "<strong>Lindsay</strong>", "<strong>Castillo</strong>" ]
```

All we want from the `object` variable here is a list of property values, which are strings, so that we can format them. In other words, the fact that the keys are `first`, `last`, and `age` is irrelevant. So first, we call `values()` to build an array of values. Next, we pass that array to `filter()`, removing anything that's not a string. We then pass the output of this to `map()`, where we're able to map the string using `<strong/>` tags.

The opposite might also be true—the value is completely meaningless without its key. If that's the case, it may be fitting to map key-value pairs to a new collection, as shown in the following example:

```
function capitalize(s) {
    return s.charAt(0).toUpperCase() + s.slice(1);
}

function format(label, value) {
    return '<label>' + capitalize(label) + ':</label>' +
        '<strong>' + value + '</strong>';
}

var object = {
    first: 'Julian',
    last: 'Ramos',
    age: 43
};

_.map(_.pairs(object), function(pair) {
    return format.apply(undefined, pair);
});
// →
// [
//   "<label>First:</label><strong>Julian</strong>",
//   "<label>Last:</label><strong>Ramos</strong>",
//   "<label>Age:</label><strong>43</strong>"
// ]
```

We're passing the result of running our object through the `pairs()` function to `map()`. The argument passed to our `map` callback function is an array, the first element being the key and the second being the value. It so happens that the `format()` function expects a key and a value to format the given string, so we're able to use `format.apply()` to call the function, passing it the `pair` array. This approach is just a matter of taste. There's no need to call `pairs()` before `map()`. We could just as easily have called `format` directly. But sometimes, this approach is preferred, and the reasons, not least of which is the style of the programmer, are wide and varied.

Reducing collections

It's now time to look at reducing collections. Lo-Dash helps a lot here too, supplying functions that help us reduce arrays, objects, and anything that's thrown our way. Aside from primitives, all data structures can be reduced to something simpler.

We'll start off by looking at the common reduce cases, summing values, and such. This will be followed by the topic of filtering collections and how it relates to reducing. Then, we'll look at some more advanced computational techniques.

Summing values

Unlike other programming languages, JavaScript has no built-in mechanism to sum together an array of values. The closest we get to summing is the native `Array.reduce()` method, which is actually general purpose and not specifically for summing values. The Lo-Dash version of `reduce` is even more general purpose, and here's an example of how to use it in summing values in a collection:

```
var collection = [
    { ram: 1024, storage: 2048 },
    { ram: 2048, storage: 4096 },
    { ram: 1024, storage: 2048 },
    { ram: 2048, storage: 4096 }
];

_.reduce(collection, function(result, item) {
    return result + item.ram;
}, 0);
// → 6144

_.reduce(collection, function(result, item) {
```

```
    return result + item.storage;
}, 0);
// → 12288
```

Here, we have a simple collection that we're reducing to two values. The first call to `reduce()` has a callback that sums together the **accumulator** and the `ram` property of the current item. The second `reduce()` call does the same thing, except that it works on the `storage` property. We're essentially reducing the collection to a number, hence the term. You'll also notice that we passed a `0` value to `reduce()` after the callback function. This is the accumulator. As the name suggests, its job is to accumulate data as each item is passed through the callback. This is also called the result and is always passed as the first argument to the `reduce` callback. Let's look at a different kind of accumulator now:

```
var collection = [
    { hits: 2, misses: 4 },
    { hits: 5, misses: 1 },
    { hits: 3, misses: 8 },
    { hits: 7, misses: 3 }
];

_.reduce(collection, function(result, item) {
    return {
        hits: result.hits + item.hits,
        misses: result.misses + item.misses
    };
}, { hits: 0, misses: 0 });
// → { hits: 17, misses: 16 }
```

This accumulator is an object and it initializes two properties to `0`. The callback function just keeps returning a new accumulator object with computed sums of `hits` and `misses`. A nice side effect to this approach is that there's only one call to `reduce()` instead of two. However, accumulators aren't strictly necessary. In simple cases of summing items, there's actually no point in using them. This is shown in the following code:

```
function add(a, b) {
    return a + b;
}

var collection = [
    { wins: 34, loses: 21 },
    { wins: 58, loses: 12 },
```

```
        { wins: 34, loses: 23 },
        { wins: 40, loses: 15 }
    ];

    _.reduce(_.range(1, 6), add);
    // → 15

    _.reduce(_.pluck(collection, 'wins'), add);
    // → 166

    _.reduce(_.pluck(collection, 'loses'), add);
    // → 71
```

This example uses a generic `reduce` callback function that returns the sum of its two arguments. Then we have a basic collection of objects, each with two properties. The first call to `reduce()` passes an array of numbers to the `add()` callback. The next two calls first use `pluck()` to build an array of numbers, using their respective key name strings. These calls use the same callback. The thing to notice about this code is that there is no explicit accumulator in the call to `reduce()`. The default, when none is specified by the caller, is the first element of the collection. With arrays that have primitive values such as these, this is fine and can actually simplify the callback function.

Filtering and reducing

You won't always need or want to reduce entire collections to a single value. Instead, it's a filtered subset that's required. Sometimes, your code is passed a collection that's the result of applying a filter to some larger collection. Or, you need to apply the filter itself. Consider the following code:

```
var collection = [
    { name: 'Gina', age: 34, enabled: true },
    { name: 'Trevor', age: 45, enabled: false },
    { name: 'Judy', age: 71, enabled: true },
    { name: 'Preston', age: 19, enabled: false }
];

_.reduce(_.filter(collection, 'enabled'), function(result, item) {
    result.names.push(item.name);
    result.years += item.age;
    return result;
}, { names: [], years: 0 });
// →
// {
```

```
//   names: [
//     "Gina",
//     "Judy"
//   ],
//   years: 105
// }
```

The `filter()` function is used only to feed enabled objects to the `reduce()` call. This is called filtering *then* reducing. However, there's an alternative approach that could be applied here. This is shown in the following code:

```
var collection = [
    { name: 'Melissa', age: 28, enabled: true },
    { name: 'Kristy', age: 22, enabled: true },
    { name: 'Kerry', age: 31, enabled: false },
    { name: 'Damon', age: 36, enabled: false }
];

_.reduce(collection, function(result, item) {
    if (item.enabled) {
        result.names.push(item.name);
        result.years += item.age;
    }
    return result;
}, { names: [], years: 0 });
// →
// {
//   names: [
//     "Melissa",
//     "Kristy"
//   ],
//   years: 50
// }
```

This approach performs the necessary filtering inside the callback. This is called filtering *and* reducing. If the item isn't enabled, we simply return the last result. If it's enabled, we do the regular reduce work. So it's as though we're simply skipping items that would have been filtered anyway. This has the advantage that with big collections, you're not doing a linear operation through the collection twice, but only once. The downside is the added complexity in the `reduce` callback. But wherever this can be minimized, such as in the preceding case, shift the filtering work to the `reduce` callback to optimize your code.

Min, max, and average operations

Lo-Dash has functions that help in more complex operations and simultaneously let you write clean and concise code. For example, the `min()` and `max()` functions accept callbacks that let them be used in a variety of situations, as shown in the following example:

```
function score(item) {
    return _.reduce(item.scores, function(result, score) {
        return result + score;
    });
}

var collection = [
    { name: 'Madeline', scores: [ 88, 45, 83 ] },
    { name: 'Susan', scores: [ 79, 82, 78 ] },
    { name: 'Hugo', scores: [ 90, 84, 85 ] },
    { name: 'Thomas', scores: [ 74, 69, 78 ] }
];

_.min(collection, score);
// →
// {
//   name: "Madeline",
//   scores: [
//     88,
//     45,
//     83
//   ]
// }

_.max(collection, score);
// →
// {
//   name: "Hugo",
//   scores: [
//     90,
//     84,
//     85
//   ]
// }
```

The `score()` function defined in this code reduces the passed-in item to the sum of its `scores` property, assumed to be an array. This is meant to be used as a callback to the `min()` and `max()` functions. The idea is that `score()` is applied to each object in our collection and the minimum or maximum value is returned. So we're actually doing two reduce jobs, one for the `scores` property and another for the collection.

Reducing collections to averages is a little trickier because there's no Lo-Dash function called `avg()` that reduces a collection to an average. Let's see if we can implement something that doesn't require much more code than the preceding example:

```
function average(items) {
    return _.reduce(items, function(result, item) {
        return result + item;
    }) / items.length;
}

var collection = [
    { name: 'Anthony', scores: [ 89, 59, 78 ] },
    { name: 'Wendy', scores: [ 84, 80, 81 ] },
    { name: 'Marie', scores: [ 58, 67, 63 ] },
    { name: 'Joshua', scores: [ 76, 68, 74 ] }
];

_.reduce(collection, function(result, item, index, coll) {
    var ave = average(item.scores);
    result.push(ave);
    if (index === (coll.length - 1)) {
        return average(result);
    }
    return result;
}, []).toFixed(2);
// → "73.08"
```

Like the `scores()` callback function before this example, we have an `average()` function. This reduces the passed-in items to their average value. Our collection is composed of objects, each of which has a `scores` array. We're interested in finding the average of the entire collection. So, we'll call `reduce()` on our collection. The callback uses the `average()` function to compute the average score for each item. This result is then added to the `reduce()` accumulator. If we've reached the last item, average is done by checking the collection length. Then it's time to compute the final average—an average of averages. Since the accumulator is an array of numbers, we can simply return the value generated by passing it to `average()`.

Reducing objects

In this section, we will turn our attention to reducing objects and working with object accumulators. Reducing objects is a lot like reducing arrays, the difference being that you have a key instead of an index. Oh yeah, there's also the ordering, which is kind of important—arrays are ordered, objects aren't.

Previously in the chapter, we caught a glimpse of what accumulators are. Here we'll take a deeper look at object accumulators, including some of the built-in Lo-Dash functions that utilize this concept.

Reducing keys

You can reduce an object to something different based solely on its keys. For example, if there are only certain properties you need, you can reduce the object to include only those properties, using the following code:

```
var object = {
        first: 'Kerry',
        last: 'Singleton',
        age: 41
    },
    allowed = [ 'first', 'last' ];

_.reduce(object, function(result, value, key) {
    if (_.contains(allowed, key)) {
        result[key] = value;
    }
    return result;
}, {});
// → { first: "Kerry", last: "Singleton" }

_.pick(object, allowed);
// → { first: "Kerry", last: "Singleton" }
```

The `allowed` array contains the names of allowed property keys, and we're using the `reduce()` function to check whether the given key is allowed or not. If it is allowed, it gets added to the object accumulator. Otherwise, it's skipped. You'll notice that we can achieve the same effect by passing the `allowed` array to the `pick()` function. So check what Lo-Dash does out of the box before writing your own callback. On the other hand, your own code lends itself to changeability.

Object accumulators

As an alternative to `reduce()`, the `transform()` function is used to transform a source object into a target object. The main difference is that with `transform`, there's an implied accumulator. This accumulator object is created when the `transform()` function is first called. It's then passed as a reference to the `callback` function for each property, as shown in the following example:

```
var object = {
    first: '&lt;strong&gt;Nicole&lt;/strong&gt;',
    last: '&lt;strong&gt;Russel&lt;/strong&gt;',
    age: 26
};

_.transform(object, function(result, value, key) {
    if (_.isString(value)) {
        result[key] = _.unescape(value);
    }
});
// →
// {
//   first: "<strong>Nicole</strong>",
//   last: "<strong>Russel</strong>"
// }
```

Here we have an object with two string properties. The `callback` function we passed to `transform()` looks for string properties and uses `unescape()` to replace any HTML character codes. The `result` argument is here, just as it was in the `reduce()` callbacks, but we don't need to return it. We also don't need to supply an accumulator object because it is created for us. Let's take a closer look at how the accumulator is created.

> The downside to using `transform()` is that it looks as though you're transforming and returning the object that was passed in, which isn't the case. The `transform()` function does not touch the source object.

Let's say we're transforming an instance of a class, rather than just a plain object. This can be done using the following code:

```
function Person(first, last) {
    this.first = first;
```

```
        this.last = last;
    }

    Person.prototype.name = function name() {
        return this.first + ' ' + this.last;
    };

    var object = new Person('Alex', 'Rivera');

    _.transform(object, function(result, value, key) {
        if (_.isString(value)) {
            result[key] = value.toUpperCase();
        }
    }).name();
    // → "ALEX RIVERA"
```

The `object` variable holds an instance of `Person`. Our `transform()` callback simply looks for strings and transforms them into their uppercase equivalents. When we call the `name()` function on the transformed object, we get the uppercase result we expect. Notice that the `name()` method is on the `Person` prototype. The `transform()` function constructs the transformed instance properly using the appropriate constructor function. This ensures that the prototypical methods and properties are where they should be.

Lo-Dash has other functions that work along the same lines in terms of object accumulators, the difference being that the source is a collection instead of an object. For example, you can take a collection and group or index the items, as shown in the following code:

```
var collection = [
    { id: _.uniqueId('id-'), position: 'absolute', top: 12 },
    { id: _.uniqueId('id-'), position: 'relative', top: 20 },
    { id: _.uniqueId('id-'), position: 'absolute', top: 12 },
    { id: _.uniqueId('id-'), position: 'relative', top: 20 }
];

_.groupBy(collection, 'position');
// →
// {
//   absolute: [
//     { id: "id-1", position: "absolute", top: 12 },
```

```
//     { id: "id-3", position: "absolute", top: 12 }
//   ],
//   relative: [
//     { id: "id-2", position: "relative", top: 20 },
//     { id: "id-4", position: "relative", top: 20 }
//   ]
// }

_.indexBy(collection, 'id');
// →
// {
//   "id-1": {
//     id: "id-1",
//     position: "absolute",
//     top: 12
//   },
//   "id-2": {
//     id: "id-2",
//     position: "relative",
//     top: 20
//   },
//   "id-3": {
//     id: "id-3",
//     position: "absolute",
//     top: 12
//   },
//   "id-4": {
//     id: "id-4",
//     position: "relative",
//     top: 20
//   }
// }
```

The `groupBy()` function groups items of the collection according to the value of the specified property. That is, if the same two items have the same `position` property value, they'll be grouped together under the same object key. On the other hand, `indexBy()` will put only one item in a given key. So this function is better suited for unique properties such as identifiers. Instead of a `property` string, we can pass a function that generates the value if we're so inclined. The result of running the `indexBy()` call is an object with unique keys that we can use to look up items.

Binding contexts

You might not always want to use anonymous functions, or Lo-Dash functions, as your `map()` callback. This is the same case with `reduce()`. Luckily, you can easily bind the callback function context in both cases. For example, let's say that you have an application object that is not global. You can still make it the context of your callback function, as shown in the following code:

```
var app = {
    states: [
        'running',
        'off',
        'paused'
    ],
    machines: [
        { id: _.uniqueId(), state: 1 },
        { id: _.uniqueId(), state: 0 },
        { id: _.uniqueId(), state: 0 },
        { id: _.uniqueId(), state: 2 }
    ]
};

var mapStates = _.partialRight(_.map, function(item) {
    return _.extend({
        state: this.states[item.state]
    }, _.pick(item, 'id'));
}, app);

mapStates(app.machines);
// →
// [
//   { state: "off", id: "1" },
//   { state: "running", id: " " },
//   { state: "running", id: " " },
//   { state: "paused", id: " " }
// ]
```

The preceding example uses the `partialRight()` function to compose a callback function. We're partially applying arguments to the `map()` function. The first is the callback function and the second is the context of the function, the `app` instance in this case. This basically enables the callback function to refer to the `this` keyword as the application, despite it not being in the global scope.

The same context-binding principle can be applied to the `reduce()` function:

```
var collection = [ 12, 34, 53, 43 ],
    settings = { tax: 1.15 },
    applyTax = _.partialRight(_.reduce, function(result, item) {
        return result + item * this.tax;
    }, 0, settings);

applyTax(collection).toFixed(2);
// → "163.30"
```

Here, the `reduce` callback is a partial function that has a `settings` object as its context. This object has a `tax` property that's used to reduce the collection, by multiplying its value by each item in the collection. This result is then added to the accumulator.

Map/reduce patterns

We'll close the chapter with an introduction to some basic map/reduce patterns, applicable to everything you've learned in this chapter so far. First, we'll take a look at what generic callback functions look like and why they're useful. Then we'll introduce the notion of map/reduce chains.

Generic callback functions

As the development of your frontend application progresses, you'll start to notice that there is some commonality between all of your map/reduce callback functions. In other words, you could probably factor the generic aspects of the callbacks into a single generic callback. As you've seen throughout this chapter and the previous chapter, it's easy to partially apply and compose new functions with Lo-Dash. This is especially helpful when you have a handful of generic functions that you'd like to use as callbacks.

For instance, let's create some generic `map()` callback functions and see how they can be used:

```
function add(item) {
    var result = _.clone(item);
    result[this.prop] += this.value;
    return result;
}

function upper(item) {
```

```
        var result = _.clone(item);
        result[this.prop] = result[this.prop].toUpperCase();
        return result;
    }

    var collection = [
        { name: 'Gerard', balance: 100 },
        { name: 'Jean', balance: 150 },
        { name: 'Suzanne', balance: 200 },
        { name: 'Darrell', balance: 250 }
    ];

    var mapAdd = _.partial(_.map, collection, add),
        mapUpper = _.partial(_.map, collection, upper);

    mapAdd({ prop: 'balance', value: 50 });
    // →
    // [
    //   { name: "Gerard", balance: 150 },
    //   { name: "Jean", balance: 200 },
    //   { name: "Suzanne", balance: 250 },
    //   { name: "Darrell", balance: 300 }
    // ]

    mapAdd({ prop: 'balance', value: 100 });
    // →
    // [
    //   { name: "Gerard", balance: 200 },
    //   { name: "Jean", balance: 250 },
    //   { name: "Suzanne", balance: 300 },
    //   { name: "Darrell", balance: 350 }
    // ]

    mapUpper({ prop: 'name'});
    // →
    // [
    //   { name: "GERARD", balance: 100 },
    //   { name: "JEAN", balance: 150 },
    //   { name: "SUZANNE", balance: 200 },
    //   { name: "DARRELL", balance: 250 }
    // ]
```

Here, we have two generic functions, `add()` and `upper()`. They both follow similar patterns. For example, both refer to the `this.prop` property. So they're both context dependent. However, this is a strength, not a weakness. The `add()` callback uses `this.prop` to determine which property to manipulate. The `this.value` property determines the value to add. As we've seen, it's easy to supply context to these functions and that's how we get specific information to these callbacks. The `upper()` callback does the same thing, but it transforms the existing property to uppercase.

The `mapAdd()` and `mapUpper()` functions are created as partials, pre-supplying the collection and the generic callback function. All that's missing is the context and that is supplied when the function is called. This means these functions have the potential to be useful throughout the application, getting new contexts when called.

> It's tempting, as with any other programming endeavor to try and create generic map/reduce callback functions up-front, that is, trying to foresee where you'll need similar but slightly different functionality. The truth is that **hindsight** is a powerful tool. It's much easier to see where generic functions become useful after you've started to repeat yourself. **Foresight**, on the other hand, tends to lead to conceptually useful callback functions that aren't actually needed.

All the ideas that apply to generic functions for `map()` callback functions also apply to `reduce()` callback functions. Here's an example:

```
function sum(a, b) {
    return a + b[this.prop];
}

var collection = [
    { low: 40, high: 70 },
    { low: 43, high: 83 },
    { low: 39, high: 79 },
    { low: 45, high: 74 }
];

var reduceSum = _.partial(_.reduce, collection, sum, 0);

reduceSum({ prop: 'low' });
// → 167

reduceSum({ prop: 'high' });
// → 306
```

The generic `sum()` function returns the sum of the two arguments. However, it uses `this.prop` to determine which property should be added. Then we proceed to create the `reduceSum()` function using `partial()`. Now we can call `reduceSum()` with any context we want.

Map/reduce chains

The final pattern we'll look at in this chapter is the notion of a map/reduce chain. This is closely related to the map/reduce programming model introduced by Google. The idea is that with large datasets, it's easier to tackle computationally intensive problems when you can break the problem into a set of mapping operations. These operations are then fed to a set of reducing operations. From this perspective, it's much easier to distribute the computation across nodes.

What we're interested in, however, is the handoff that takes place between the map job and the reduce job. The map job is responsible for mapping the source data to something that is consumable by the reduce job. This pattern might actually repeat several times. For example, a dataset is mapped and then reduced. The result of reducing it is then further mapped, and further reduced, and so on. Let's see how something like this looks in Lo-Dash:

```
var collection = [
    { name: 'Wade', balance: 100 },
    { name: 'Donna', balance: 125 },
    { name: 'Glenn', balance: 90 },
    { name: 'Floyd', balance: 110 }
], bonus = 25;

var mapped = _.map(collection, function(item) {
    return _.extend({
        bonus: item.balance + bonus
    }, item);
});

_.reduce(mapped, function(result, item, index, coll) {
    result += (item.bonus - item.balance) / item.bonus;
    if (index === (coll.length - 1)) {
        result = result / coll.length * 100;
    }
    return result;
}, 0).toFixed(2) + '%';
// → "19.23%"
```

Here, we map the collection by computing the amount after adding a `bonus` property to the `balance` item for each item. This newly mapped collection is stored in the `mapped` variable. Then we reduce the collection to the average rate of increase. Note that the reduce callback expects a mapped collection since it makes use of the `bonus` property, which isn't in the original collection.

Summary

This chapter introduced you to the map/reduce programming model and how Lo-Dash tools can help to realize it in your application. First, we examined mapping collections, including how to choose which properties get included and how to perform calculations. We then moved on to mapping objects. Keys have an important role in how objects get mapped to new objects and collections. There are also methods and functions to consider when mapping.

The second part of the chapter covered reducing, including how to sum items, how to transform objects, and how to formulate generic callback functions that can be used in a variety of contexts. The chapter closed with a brief look at what chaining map/reduce operations together looks like.

Map/reduce is an important topic because Lo-Dash supports many variations of the programming model. It's now time to expand on the chaining concept, and it turns out that there's a lot more than just map/reduce functions that can be glued together.

5
Assembling Chains

So far, the examples we've looked at in this book used Lo-Dash functions independently of one another. That's not to say they're not working together; it's just that they could be cleaner, or more condensed. We would call the function to compute a value, store that value, call another function to compute a new value using the stored value as an argument, and repeat the same process. This is exhausting but can be easily remedied.

The idea is to streamline this functionality into a chain of calls. This approach follows the concept of applicative programming, whereby we have a starting collection and at each stage in the chain, that collection is transformed. It's like an assembly line where the resulting product is a value that you need in a given context.

Lo-Dash enables this mode of programming through the wrapper concept—a constructor function used to wrap primitive values that enable chained function calls. In this chapter, we'll see how we can use this approach to simplify complex code and even produce reusable components.

In this chapter, we will cover the following topics:

- Creating Lo-Dash wrappers
- Building filters
- Testing truth conditions
- Counting items
- Transformations
- Intermediary results
- Keys and values
- Returning chains

Creating Lo-Dash wrappers

In this section, we'll introduce the concept of wrapping values. Then we'll use the wrapper to chain function calls. We'll also look at how call chains are terminated.

Chained calls

Chaining function calls together is a pattern of applicative programming, where a collection is transformed into something different. This newly transformed collection is then passed to the next call in the chain, and so on. This is where the term applicative comes from; you're applying functions to every item in a collection. Since this process is repeated over and over, it's easy to package chained calls into a reusable component. It's a pipeline that's adding, removing, or modifying values along each step of the way, producing a result at the end.

Another way, perhaps, is a more practical view of chains, which is just a simpler way to make function calls. jQuery popularized this notion. When reading jQuery code, you'll find that there are a lot of chained calls, and yet the code is readable. Often, chains can be built as a single statement, as shown in the following code:

```
$('body')
    .children()
    .first()
    .is('h1');
// → true
```

This jQuery chain consists of four calls, expressed as a single statement. The first call is to the jQuery constructor, which wraps the specified DOM elements. Next, we call `children()` to get the child elements. The `first()` function returns the first child element. The chain is terminated with a call to `is()`, which returns a simple Boolean value, not a jQuery object.

> Take note of the code formatting here. If you're going to compose chains of functionality, it is important to keep your code readable. The main convention that I would recommend to follow is to indent chained calls on the next line. This way, you don't have statements that span an obnoxious number of columns, and you can tell at a glance that this chunk of code is a chain of function calls.

Wrapping values

Wrapping values in Lo-Dash works pretty much the same as with jQuery. There's a wrapper call that constructs the jQuery/Lo-Dash object. Each **chainable** call returns a wrapper object. There's a terminating call that returns a primitive type. There are some obvious differences too, with regard to how jQuery and Lo-Dash wrap values. For instance, you can't pass a CSS selector string to the Lo-Dash wrapper function and expect it to wrap DOM elements. Nor would you want it to—Lo-Dash is a low-level utility library, whereas jQuery works at a fundamentally higher level of abstraction.

That's not the whole story of how wrapping values and applying function call chains work. There are subtle nuances and edge cases around every corner, all of which we'll address over the course of the chapter. But for now, let's get into the code:

```
_(['a', 'b', 'c'])
    .at([1, 2])
    .value();
// → [ "b", "c" ]
```

Here is our hello-world chain. The _ object we've been using throughout the book to access the Lo-Dash API is also a constructor function. It takes a JavaScript primitive as an argument. This is the value that's wrapped and passed to the first function call in the chain. Here, we're calling the `at()` function, saying that we want the items at indices `1` and `2`. The call to `value()` gets us the result we're after.

The preceding code obviously doesn't warrant using a wrapper—there's only one function call. The point, however, isn't conciseness but rather the basic anatomy of a call chain. As we get to more elaborate examples throughout the chapter, we'll see how chains substantially reduce the amount of code written. Here are two more Lo-Dash wrapper constructors:

```
_({a: 'b', c: 'd'})
    .contains('b');
// → true

_('abcd')
    .contains('b');
// → true
```

The first wrapper uses a plain object as its primitive value. The second wrapper uses a string. The chain is terminated immediately in both cases because we're calling `contains()`, which itself returns a primitive Boolean value. Again, we didn't have to write the preceding code using wrappers and call chains. It's better that you don't if you're calling only one function, since you'd only be confusing other readers of your code otherwise. The point of the preceding code is to illustrate that we can wrap both plain objects and strings and treat them as collections.

Explicit and implicit chaining

Once we have a Lo-Dash wrapper instance, we can start making chained function calls. However, not all of these functions are chainable. **Non-chainable** functions return primitive values such as Booleans or numbers. This is what is referred to as implicit chaining. It's implicit because functions that would return a collection actually return a Lo-Dash wrapper instance. Other functions don't have collections as return values. Calls to these functions will terminate the chain.

On the other hand, there's explicit chaining—this will keep the chain alive until it's explicitly terminated by calling `value()`. For example, if your chain is explicit, calling `contains()` will return a wrapper, instead of a Boolean as it normally would. The following are examples of implicit and explicit chaining:

```
_([3,2,1])
    .sort()
    .first();
// → 1

_.chain([3,2,1])
    .sort()
    .first()
    .isNumber()
    .value();
// → true
```

The first chain uses the default Lo-Dash chaining configuration. The `first()` function grabs the first item in an array and returns it. Since this item could be anything (in this case, it's a number), the `first()` function isn't chainable. We don't need to make an explicit call to `value()` since functions that aren't chainable return **unwrapped** values. The second chain, however, uses explicit chaining. This is done by constructing the Lo-Dash wrapper instance with the `chain()` function. The resulting wrapper is the same in every way, except that we need to make an explicit call to `value()` to unwrap the value. With explicit chaining, every function is chainable. For example, the call to `first()` now returns a wrapper instance instead of a number. This is also done by `isNumber()`.

The main reason you would want to use explicit chains like this is to avoid temporary variables and additional statements after the chain is complete. In the explicit chain in the preceding code, for instance, we just need to know whether the first item in the sorted collection is a number or not. There's no need to store the first item in a new variable if we can get exactly what we're after from the chain.

Building filters

A powerful use of chained function calls is building filters that successively filter out unwanted items from a larger collection. Let's say that you already have a piece of code that's using the `filter()` function on a collection. But now you need to alter that filtering operation, perhaps by adding additional constraints. Rather than messing around with the existing `filter()` code that you know works, you can build a filter chain.

Multiple filter() calls

The simplest approach to assembling filter chains is to join together multiple calls to the `filter()` function. Here's an example of what that might look like:

```
var collection = [
    { name: 'Ellen', age: 20, enabled: true },
    { name: 'Heidi', age: 24, enabled: false },
    { name: 'Roy', age: 21, enabled: true },
    { name: 'Garry', age: 23, enabled: false }
];

_(collection)
    .filter('enabled')
    .filter(function(item) {
        return item.age >= 21;
    })
   .value();
// → [ { name: "Roy", age: 21, enabled: true } ]
```

The first call to `filter()` uses the pluck-style shorthand on the `enabled` property, which filters out items with false values for this property. The next call to `filter()` uses a callback function that filters out items where the `age` property value is less than `21`. We're left with a single item, which is unwrapped by calling `value()`.

> So what's the point of two or more calls to `filter()` when we could just modify the callback function? Wouldn't that mean less code and faster execution? The real advantage is in reading and modifying this code. Do we want to see what happens when we remove the enabled filter? Just comment out the line. Readability and maintainability should almost always trump attempts to squeeze performance out of complicated callback functions. Of course, there are exceptions to this, but don't invent performance issues for the sake of it.

Combining filter() with where()

The `where()` function is an expressive means to filter a collection using logical `and` conditions. Rather than trying to express all of your query constraints in a single `filter()` callback function, why not utilize the `where()` notation where it makes sense? Let's see this in action:

```
var collection = [
    { name: 'Janice', age: 38, gender: 'f' },
    { name: 'Joey', age: 20, gender: 'm' },
    { name: 'Lauren', gender: 'f' },
    { name: 'Drew', gender: 'm' }
];

_(collection)
    .where({ gender: 'f' })
    .filter(_.flow(_.property('age'), _.isFinite))
    .value();
// → [ { name: "Janice", age: 38, gender: "f" } ]
```

This filter will include all female items and is a good candidate for the `where()` function. Next, we'd like to make sure that all items have an `age` property whose value is a finite number. We do this by composing a callback function that's passed to `filter()`. We're utilizing a couple of shortcuts here instead of defining our own inline callback function. The `flow()` function will construct a function for us, letting the result flow to each function argument we give it. We use the `property()` function to build a function that gets us the `age` property for each item, and gets passed to the `isFinite()` function. There are a couple of items in our collection that don't have `age` properties. These undefined values don't pass the test and are filtered out.

> The ordering of chained filter functions can be important. For example, it's wise to filter broadly first. That way, your collection shrinks in size faster as it flows through the pipeline, which means less work for other functions. Where this matters isn't immediately apparent, but as your code matures, you'll start to notice ordering tweaks. The nice thing about chained structures in your code is that order changes are trivial.

Dropping and taking collection items

Lo-Dash has tools that let us filter collections from either the beginning or the end of a collection. These tools are especially useful in the context of function call chains, since using them usually depends on a prior transformation of the collection. For example, consider the sort order in the following code:

```
var collection = [
    { first: 'Dewey', last: 'Mills' },
    { first: 'Charlene', last: 'Larson' },
    { first: 'Myra', last: 'Gray' },
    { first: 'Tasha', last: 'Malone' }
];

_(collection)
    .sortBy('first')
    .dropWhile(function(item) {
        return _.first(item.first) < 'F';
    })
    .value();
// →
// [
//   { first: "Myra", last: "Gray" },
//   { first: "Tasha", last: "Malone" }
// ]
```

The first call in this chain sorts the collection by the `first` property using the `sortBy()` function. Now that the collection is sorted, we can call `dropWhile()`. Starting from the left-hand side, this function drops items from the collection until the callback returns `true`. Our particular callback gets the first character of the name string, and if it is less than `F`, we drop it. This leaves us with a collection that only has first names starting with `F` and above.

In addition to dropping items from the left-hand side of the collection, we can drop items from the right-hand side. Alternatively, we can combine the two approaches using a chain, as shown in the following code:

```
var name = '  Donnie Woods   ',
    emptyString = _.partial(_.isEqual, ' ');

_(name)
    .toArray()
    .dropWhile(emptyString)
    .dropRightWhile(emptyString)
    .join('');
// → "Donnie Woods"
```

Here, we're wrapping a string value instead of an array, emulating the functionality of `String.trim()`. So the first task for our chain is to use `toArray()` to split the string into individual characters. The drop functions expect an array. Next, we use the `dropWhile()` function and pass it our `emptyString()` callback function. This will drop characters from the string until it finds an actual character. It then uses `dropRightWhile()` to perform the same task but from the opposite side of the array, moving in the opposite direction. Lastly, we join the array back together as a string, minus the empty characters that have been dropped from either end.

> Yes, you can get the same result using a regular expression and condensed code. Regular expressions are great, but they're not for everyone, and they only work with strings. Weigh your options before going in either direction.

We can perform the inverse of dropping items from either end of an array. We can take items, thus dropping everything else. For example:

```
var collection = [
    { name: 'Jeannie', grade: 'B+' },
    { name: 'Jeffrey', grade: 'C' },
    { name: 'Carrie', grade: 'A-' },
    { name: 'James', grade: 'A' }
];

_(collection)
    .sortBy('grade')
    .takeWhile(function(item) {
        return _.first(item.grade) === 'A';
    })
    .value();
```

```
// →
// [
//   { name: "James", grade: "A" },
//   { name: "Carrie", grade: "A-" }
// ]
```

We're only interested in items with `A` grades. The callback function we're using with `takeWhile()` returns `true` for items that have an `A`. Of course, this only works because the first step in the chain was to sort the array by the `grade` property. Had we not done that first, we would end up missing the items we're looking for.

Items can also be taken from the collection in the opposite direction. That is, instead of moving from left to right, we move from right to left. This is ideal when ordering is important and you don't want to perform additional steps to take what you need from the collection. This ordering is shown in the following code:

```
var collection = _.sample(_.range(1, 21), 10),
    total = 5,
    min = 10;

_(collection)
    .sortBy()
    .takeRightWhile(function(item, index, array) {
        return item >= min &&
            array.length - index <= total;
    })
    .value();
// → [ 13, 14, 15, 17, 20 ]
```

The collection used here is a random sampling of 10 integers. The first call in our chain is to `sortBy()`, which simply sorts the array with no arguments supplied. This is in ascending order and we want the top five items. We could have reversed the sort order, but instead, we're skipping that step and jumping right into the `takeRightWhile()` function. The callback used here will return numbers as long as the number is larger than `min` and as long as we haven't exceeded the total.

Rejecting items

Rejecting works much in the same way as filtering does. In the case of filtering, you know what you want. In the case of rejecting, you know what you don't want. These rejection operations can be chained together to build complex queries, as shown in the following code:

```
var object = {
    first: 'Conrad',
```

```
        last: 'Casey',
        age: 37,
        enabled: true
};

_(object)
    .reject(_.isBoolean)
    .reject(_.isString)
    .first()
    .toFixed(2);
// → "37.00"
```

Here we're chaining together two `reject()` calls. The wrapped value is an object and we're only after those property values that aren't Booleans or strings. These functions—`isBoolean()` and `isString()`—already exist as a part of the Lo-Dash API, and we can just pass them directly to `reject()`. There's no need to write our own callback functions here.

We can use the `result()` function to help us reject collection items in a chain. The `result()` function works in the same way, whether the specified property value is a function or a non-callable value. Here's an illustration of the differences in calling `reject()` using `result()` or just a property name:

```
function User(name, disabled) {
    this.name = name;
    this.disabled = disabled;
}

User.prototype.enabled = function() {
    return !this.disabled;
};

var collection = [
        new User('Phil', true),
        new User('Wilson', false),
        new User('Kathey', true),
        new User('Nina', false)
    ],
    enabled = _.flow(_.identity,
        _.partialRight(_.result, 'enabled'));

_(collection)
    .reject('disabled')
```

```
        .value();
// →
// [
//   { name: "Wilson", disabled: false },
//   { name: "Nina", disabled: false }
// ]

_(collection)
    .reject(_.negate(enabled))
    .value();
// →
// [
//   { name: "Wilson", disabled: false },
//   { name: "Nina", disabled: false }
// ]
```

The `User` instances have a `disabled` property, and the `enabled()` method returns `true` if `disabled` is false. The `collection` variable holds an array of these `User` instances. The `enabled()` function is something we construct ourselves. We'll use it as a callback with `reject()`. This function uses `result()` to get the `enabled()` value from each item in the collection. The `identity()` function is used here as a trick to get `partialRight()` to work as a callback for `reject()`.

Using initial() and rest()

The `initial()` function takes everything but the last element—this can be combined with chained operations in interesting ways. For example, let's say we have a simple string we need to clean up:

```
var string = 'abc\n';

_(string)
    .slice()
    .initial()
    .join('');
// → "abc"
```

If we know the string is always going to end with something we don't care about, this is an easy way to drop that off. The same code works with arrays too; we're not limiting ourselves to strings. For example, the `slice()` function is a part of the chain and it makes the chain work with strings. If we passed an array, `slice()` wouldn't have any impact—the same code would still work. However, we might want to remove it later on, along with the `join()` call. Given the way our chain code is formatted, this is simple to do.

The inverse of `initial()` is `rest()`—it takes everything in the array but the first item. Just like the case in which we don't care about the last item, there could be cases where we don't care about the first item. An illustration of using `rest()` is as follows:

```
var collection = [
    { name: 'init', task: _.noop },
    { name: 'sort', task: _.random },
    { name: 'search', task: _.random }
];

_(collection)
    .rest()
    .invoke('task')
    .value();
// → [ 1, 1 ]
```

This collection has objects with `task()` methods. The collection is ordered, so the first task is always going to be the `init` task, which we don't care about because it's a `noop()` function. We test this by chaining `invoke()` to the `rest()` function, which if all goes well, we should end up with an array of random numbers, and no undefined values.

Testing truth conditions

Beyond simply filtering collections, you often need to test a condition of a collection. This could include filtering a collection, and then answering a simple yes/no about the results. In those cases where you need to check a truth condition of a collection, it's often easier to perform the test at the end of a chain. There's usually no need to write several statements and allocate several variables along the way.

Testing if a collection contains an item

Perhaps, the most straightforward test we can perform is whether or not a collection contains an item we're looking for. The `contains()` function is handy in cases like these because it is easy to attach to the end of a chain that's performing some other operations beforehand. One use of `contains()` is shown in the following example:

```
var string = 'abc123',
    array = [ 'a', 'b', 'c', 1, 2, 3 ];

_(string)
    .filter(_.isString)
```

```
        .contains('c');
// → true

_(array)
        .filter(_.isString)
        .contains('c');
// → true
```

There are two collections in the code—a string and an array. Both chains that follow are identical, aside from wrapping different values. However, both return `true` in this case, since the string has `c` and so does the array.

It's always good practice to use functions such as `contains()` if all you care about is testing for the item's existence. These functions will stop looping early, or short-circuit, if a value is found, saving valuable CPU cycles.

Often, you don't have the exact value. Instead you have query constraints but you're still only interested in whether they're satisfied, and not the data itself. This can be accomplished using the `find()` and `filter()` methods:

```
var string = 'Dana Porter',
    array = [
        { name: 'Luis', gender: 'm' },
        { name: 'Rhonda', gender: 'f' },
        { name: 'Kirk', gender: 'm' },
        { name: 'Emily', gender: 'f' }
    ];

_(string)
    .chain()
    .filter(function(item) {
        return item.toUpperCase() === 'A';
    })
    .size()
    .isEqual(2)
    .value();
// → true

!!(_(array)
    .find(function(item) {
        return _.first(item.name).toUpperCase() === 'R' &&
            item.gender === 'f';
    }));
// → true
```

The first chain in this code is for a string value. Notice how we've used `chain()` here to enable explicit chaining—meaning we'll have to explicitly call `value()` at the end to unwrap the result. The `filter()` call here returns items that match `A`. We do this so that we can count how many of them there are in the chain. In this case, the string passes the test because there are two `A` characters. The downside is that we're looking for an exact number—`2`. The `filter()` function will keep filtering away long after we've found two items.

The second chain uses a wrapped array. Here we're transforming the result of calling `find()` into a Boolean value. Here we're able to use more elaborate query conditions.

Everything or anything is true

Our final look at checking truth conditions in this chapter involves validating either one item at least or the collection in its entirety. That is, a collection might be considered valid if one or more items pass the test we give it. Or perhaps the requirements are more stringent and every item in the collection must pass the test in order to be considered valid. Let's see how these tests can be used in chains:

```
var collection = [
    1414728000000,
    1383192000000,
    1351656000000,
    1320033600000
];

_(collection)
    .map(function(item) {
        return new Date(item);
    })
    .every(function(item) {
        return item.getMonth() === 9 && item.getDate() === 31;
    });
// → true
```

This collection contains timestamp numbers, and so the first call in the chain is to `map()`, transforming each collection item into a `Date` instance. Now that every item is a date, we can use `every()` to validate that in this collection, every day is Halloween.

Now let's look at using the `some()` function to terminate a chain. This will validate that at least one item passes the test and will stop looping as soon as one is found:

```
var collection = [
    { name: 'Danielle', age: 34, skill: 'Backbone' },
```

```
        { name: 'Sammy', age: 19, skill: 'Ember' },
        { name: 'Donna', age: 41, skill: 'Angular' },
        { name: 'George', age: 17, skill: 'Marionette' }
    ];

    _(collection)
        .reject({ skill: 'Ember' })
        .reject({ skill: 'Angular' })
        .some(function(item) {
            return item.age >= 25;
        });
    // → true
```

You can see that after rejecting `Ember` and `Angular` enthusiasts, we make sure that there's at least one `Backbone` or `Marionette` programmer who is at least `25` years old.

Counting items

A variation on the previous topic—*Testing truth conditions*—is counting items in a collection after their values have moved through a processing chain. For example, we might need to know how many items in a collection meet the given criteria. We can get that number using a call chain.

Using length and size()

The `size()` function is handy because we can call it directly on a Lo-Dash wrapper. This is the preferred way to count the resulting items in our collection after our chain runs:

```
var object = { first: 'Charlotte', last: 'Hall' },
    array = _.range(10);

_(object)
    .omit('first')
    .size();
// → 1

_(array)
    .drop(5)
    .size();
// → 5
```

Here, we have `array` and `object`. The first chain uses the `size()` function to count the number of properties after omitting the `first` property. The second chain wraps the array and, after dropping `5` items, counts what's left.

> We can use the `length` property, but we have to call `value()` first. Using `size()` is just a shortcut.

Grouping using countBy()

We can also count more than one item. That is, given a collection, we can divide it into groups and then count the number of items in each group. Using chains, we can write some fairly sophisticated code:

```
var collection = [
    { name: 'Pamela', gender: 'f' },
    { name: 'Vanessa', gender: 'f' },
    { name: 'Gina', gender: 'f' },
    { name: 'Dennis', gender: 'm' }
];

_(collection)
    .countBy('gender')
    .pairs()
    .sortBy(1)
    .reverse()
    .pluck(0)
    .value();
// → [ "f", "m" ]
```

This chain kicks off by grouping the collection by the `gender` property. Next, we use the `pairs()` function to get an array of arrays. We do this so that we can sort the groups by the number of items in them. With the collection sorted, we can pluck the values we're interested in. In this case, the `f` gender is first since that group has a higher count.

> The preceding code uses two interesting tricks. Firstly, we're passing a numerical index to the `sortBy()` function. Since keys are accessed in the same way as indices, this works as expected. Secondly, we're passing a numerical index to the `pluck()` function and this works for the same reason as the `sortBy()` function.

Reducing collections

Our final approach to counting items in chaining operations is to reduce the collection. This is useful when you want to reduce the entire collection to a sum computed using more involved functions that are applied to each item. Collections can be reduced with the following code:

```
var collection = [
    { name: 'Chad', skills: [ 'backbone', 'lodash' ] },
    { name: 'Simon', skills: [ 'html', 'css', 'less' ] },
    { name: 'Katie', skills: [ 'grunt', 'underscore' ] },
    { name: 'Jennifer', skills: [ 'css', 'grunt', 'less' ] }
];

_(collection)
    .pluck('skills')
    .reduce(function(result, item) {
        return _.size(item) > 2 &&
            _.contains(item, 'grunt') &&
            result + 1;
    }, 0);
// → 1
```

Here, we're plucking the `skills` property from each item in the collection. We're interested in knowing two things about the `skills` value: does it contain the string `grunt`? And does it have more than `2` items? If these criteria are met, then we increment the reduced sum value that's returned by the `reduce()` call.

Transformations

Now it's time for us to look at transformations that happen to data as it passes through the processing pipelines we construct. What's interesting about Lo-Dash and how it transforms data in chains is that the original collection isn't modified—a new one is constructed. This reduces side effects and is fundamental to the immutability concept in other functional programming languages.

Building groups, unions, and unique values

Some of the most powerful transformation tools found in Lo-Dash can be used out of the box with very little effort. These include grouping collection items by a specific value they contain, joining arrays together while retaining only unique values, and removing any duplicates from arrays. For example:

```
var collection = [
    { name: 'Rudolph', age: 24 },
    { name: 'Charles', age: 43 },
    { name: 'Rodney', age: 37 },
    { name: 'Marie', age: 28 }
];

_(collection)
    .map(function(item) {
        var experience = 'seasoned veteran';
        if (item.age < 30) {
            experience = 'noob';
        } else if (item.age < 40) {
            experience = 'geek cred';
        }
        return _.extend({
            experience: experience
        }, item);
    })
    .groupBy('experience')
    .map(function(item, key) {
        return key +
            ' (' + _.pluck(item, 'name').join(', ') + ')';
    })
    .value();
// →
// [
//   "noob (Rudolph, Marie)",
//   "seasoned veteran (Charles)",
//   "geek cred (Rodney)"
// ]
```

This chain wraps a collection of plain objects, and the first call in the chain maps the `item` object to an extended version of it. We're calculating a string version of their `experience` property and assigning that to a new property. Next, we use the `groupBy()` function to group the collection by this new `experience` property. The last step in this chain is to use `map()` again to generate a string representation of the various experience groups.

Using `union()` to join arrays together can come in handy if you've already got a wrapped array and you need to ensure it has certain values, but also ensure that those values aren't duplicated. The application of `union()` is shown in the following example:

```
var collection = _.sample(_.range(1, 101), 10);

_(collection)
    .union([ 25, 50, 75])
    .sortBy()
    .value();
// → [ 1, 3, 21, 25, 27, 37, 40, 50, 57, 73, 75, 94 ]
```

You can see that our wrapped array, a sampling of 10 random numbers, is joined with another array using the `union()` function. We then return the sorted result. If you examine the output, you'll notice it'll always have `25`, `50`, and `75`. You'll also notice that these numbers are never duplicated.

Finally, if you have a collection of values and you just need the duplicates removed, the `uniq()` function allows you to do that as a step in your chained processing:

```
function name(item) {
    return item.first + ' ' + item.last;
}

var collection = [
    { first: 'Renee', last: 'Morris' },
    { first: 'Casey', last: 'Wise' },
    { first: 'Virginia', last: 'Grant' },
    { first: 'Toni', last: 'Morris' }
];

_(collection)
    .uniq('last')
    .sortBy('last')
    .value();
// →
// [
//   { first: "Virginia", last: "Grant" },
//   { first: "Renee", last: "Morris" },
//   { first: "Casey", last: "Wise" }
// ]

_(collection)
    .uniq(name)
    .sortBy(name)
```

```
        .value();
// →
// [
//   { first: "Casey", last: "Wise" },
//   { first: "Renee", last: "Morris" },
//   { first: "Toni", last: "Morris" },
//   { first: "Virginia", last: "Grant" }
// ]

_(collection)
        .map(name)
        .uniq()
        .sortBy()
        .value();
// →
// [
//   "Casey Wise",
//   "Renee Morris",
//   "Toni Morris",
//   "Virginia Grant"
// ]
```

We're seeing three different approaches to extracting the unique values from the wrapped collection. The first uses the pluck-style shorthand to filter out duplicates. Since we passed it the string `last`, it'll look for unique values in this property. The second approach passes in a callback function, which joins together the `first` and the `last` name properties. Note that this same function is used by the `sortBy()` call in the same chain. The last approach doesn't pass any arguments to `uniq()` because the first step in the chain maps our array of objects to an array of strings.

Plucking values

Often, within your chains of functionality, you'll realize that you don't need the entirety of every object in your collection. This can make what you're doing later on in the chain much simpler. To pluck values, the following code can be used:

```
var collection = [
    { gender: 'f', dob: new Date(1984, 3, 8) },
    { gender: 'm', dob: new Date(1983, 7, 16) },
    { gender: 'f', dob: new Date(1987, 2, 4) },
    { gender: 'm', dob: new Date(1988, 5, 2) }
];

_(collection)
    .where({ gender: 'm' })
```

```
    .pluck('dob')
    .map(function(item) {
        return item.toLocaleString();
    })
    .value();
// → [ "8/16/1983, 12:00:00 AM", "6/2/1988, 12:00:00 AM" ]
```

Here, we're plucking the `dob` property values and this simplifies the `map()` handler that follows in the chain. Instead of having to look up the `dob` property, the item itself is the `dob` property value.

Creating arrays using without()

If we need a new array constructed and there are certain values we know should not be present as items, we can use the `without()` function. This is typically the first action in a chain, since it creates a new array, but it's not always the first. Let's see an example of this:

```
var collection = _.range(1, 11);

return _(collection)
    .without(5, _.first(collection), _.last(collection))
    .reverse()
    .value();
// → [ 9, 8, 7, 6, 4, 3, 2 ]
```

The wrapped collection in this code includes the numbers `1` through `10`. The first call in our chain copies the items out of this array and places them in a new array, aside from the argument values passed to the `without()` function. These are not included in the new array.

Finding the min and max values

With every collection, there's a minimum and a maximum value. Finding these values with Lo-Dash is easy; you just have to use the respective `min()` and `max()` functions. But what if you need to adjust the range for which you're seeking out the minimum values? Let's use the following code to perform this task:

```
var collection = [
    { name: 'Daisy', wins: 10 },
    { name: 'Norman', wins: 12 },
    { name: 'Kim', wins: 8 },
    { name: 'Colin', wins: 4 }
];

_(collection)
```

```
    .reject(function(item) {
        return item.wins < 5
    })
    .min('wins');
// → { name: "Kim", wins: 8 }
```

In this example, we're not concerned with items that have a `win` count of less than `5`. So we know that the absolute minimum returned by this code will have `5` wins or more. After the invalid `win` counts have been rejected, we use the pluck style shorthand to find the minimum value based on the `wins` property.

The `max()` function can be used as a chain operation in a similar fashion:

```
var collection = [
    { name: 'Kerry', balance: 500, credit: 344 },
    { name: 'Franklin', balance: 0, credit: 554 },
    { name: 'Lillie', balance: 1098, credit: 50 },
    { name: 'Clyde', balance: 473, credit: -900 }
];

_(collection)
    .filter('balance')
    .filter('credit')
    .max(function(item) {
        return item.balance + item.credit;
    });
// → { name: "Lillie", balance: 1098, credit: 50 }
```

This collection has objects with the `balance` and `credit` properties. The first two chain operations use the `filter()` function to remove objects where either of these fields is false. The `max()` function then closes the chain. This time, we're using a callback function that allows us to map the values we want to compare in order to figure out the maximum value.

Finding the index

Finding the index of a given element has its uses, and we can apply the `index()` function as a step in a call chain:

```
function rank(coll, name) {
    return _(coll)
        .sortBy('score')
        .reverse()
        .pluck('name')
        .indexOf(name) + 1;
```

```
}

var collection = [
    { name: 'Ruby', score: 43 },
    { name: 'Robert', score: 59 },
    { name: 'Lindsey', score: 38 },
    { name: 'Marty', score: 55 }
];

rank(collection, 'Ruby');
// → 3

rank(collection, 'Marty');
// → 2
```

The `rank()` function in this code accepts a `collection` argument and a `name` string. The function wraps the collection and uses a call chain to figure out the rank of the passed-in name, based on the `score` property. The first step is to sort the collection and then to reverse it so that it's in descending order based on the `score` property value. Next, we pluck the names from the collection, using the `pluck()` function, which maintains the sort order we just created. Now we can use `indexOf()` to figure out the rank of the given user.

Using difference() and xor()

The last section of the transformations topic is using the `difference()` and the `xor()` functions to merge together the contents of two arrays. Both work similarly but with subtle differences that are worth noting and paying attention to. These functions are useful at the start of chains where you have to make sure that the wrapped array has only the necessary values. For example, let's say your array of numbers shouldn't have any odd values. Then we can use the following code for this condition:

```
var collection = _.range(1, 51),
    odds = _.filter(_.range(1, 101), function(item) {
        return item % 2;
    });

_(collection)
    .difference(odds)
    .takeRight(10)
    .reverse()
    .value();
// → [ 32, 34, 36, 38, 40, 42, 44, 46, 48, 50 ]
```

Our collection in this code consists of `50` numbers and the `odds` array contains odd numbers from `1` to `100`. Our chain starts off by calling the `difference()` function, passing in the `odds` array as an argument. Next, we take the top 10 items from the resulting array and sort them. The thing to notice about the result is that there are no values above 50 present. We've removed all odd numbers below 50, since that is the difference between the wrapped array and the array that was supplied as an argument. In other words, it's not a symmetrical difference. For that, we would use the `xor()` function in our chain:

```
var collection = _.range(1, 26),
    evens = _.reject(_.range(1, 51), function(item) {
        return item % 2;
    });

_(collection)
    .xor(evens)
    .reverse()
    .value();
// →
// [ 50, 48, 46, 44, 42, 40, 38, 36, 34, 32, 30, 28, 26,
//   25, 23, 21, 19, 17, 15, 13, 11, 9, 7, 5, 3, 1 ]
```

This time, our collection is an array of numbers from `1` to `25` and the `evens` array holds even numbers from `2` to `50`. We're using the `xor()` function in our chain to join the collection with the `evens` array. The difference between this and the `difference()` function is that it'll include all the values in the `evens` array that go beyond `25`, since `xor()` will compute the symmetrical difference.

Intermediary results

There are times when we don't want to wait until the call chain is terminated to have access to values computed at any given step along the way. Think about cases where the intermediate value produced by a function in the chain should be used by another function later in the chain. On other occasions, we need to completely override the value returned by the chain.

Tapping into chains

We can use the `tap()` function to inject our own callback function into the chain. This is different from the callbacks that we'd supply to other Lo-Dash functions. It doesn't alter the value as it flows through the chain of function calls. Instead, think of `tap()` as a way of intercepting values as they flow through the chain, and possibly reacting to them in some way. Let's see an example of this function:

```
var collection = [
        { name: 'Stuart', age: 41 },
        { name: 'Leah', age: 26 },
        { name: 'Priscilla', age: 37 },
        { name: 'Perry', age: 31 }
    ],
    min,
    max;

_(collection)
    .filter(function(item) {
        return item.age >= 30;
    })
    .tap(function(coll) {
        min = _.min(coll, 'age'),
        max = _.max(coll, 'age')
    })
    .reject(function(item) {
        return item.age === max.age;
    })
    .value();
// min → { name: "Perry", age: 31 }
// max → { name: "Stuart", age: 41 }
// →
// [
//   { name: "Priscilla", age: 37 },
//   { name: "Perry", age: 31 }
// ]
```

This code wraps our collection and filters out items younger than 30. Next, we use a `tap()` callback to set up our `min` and `max` variables. Note the scope of these variables; they're defined outside the chain, and are thus accessible to any future callbacks in the chain. And that's what we're doing here—we're rejecting any items where the `age` property equals the `max` age found. Note that the `max` value could turn out differently had we not computed it after the first filter in the chain.

> The only downside to this approach is that our chain is no longer a tightly encapsulated unit that can be moved around in our code. However, the trade-off is that we can elegantly compute the values needed for our chain on the fly. Something to keep in mind anyway, different programming styles may lean closer to one direction than others.

Injecting values

The other approach to manipulating what chains return at runtime is by using the `thru()` function. It behaves just like `tap()` but whatever is returned by this function becomes the new value:

```
var collection = _.range(1, _.random(11)),
    result;

result = _(collection)
     .thru(function(coll) {
         return _.size(coll) > 5 ? coll : [];
     })
     .reverse()
     .value();

_.isEmpty(result) ? 'No Results' : result.join(',');
// → "No Results"
```

This chain is kicked off using the `thru()` function callback to validate the minimum size of the collection. If it is less than `5`, we don't even have to bother—we just return an empty array. It's important that we return something that'll work with the remaining chained functions, and an empty array fits the bill nicely. We're simply using `thru()` to state that any length less than `5` should have the same meaning as an empty array. This function is actually an ideal place in which to inject these nuanced business rules that often surface well after code is written.

Keys and values

Now it's time to turn our attention to object keys and values and how they can be used in function call chains. Often, these involve wrapping a plain object in a Lo-Dash instance and then using the `keys()` or `values()` functions to bootstrap the processing. There are also times when you have a collection of objects and you want to work with certain property values only. For this purpose, there are the `pick()` and `omit()` functions that can be exercised in chains.

Filtered keys and values

We can use the result of a filtered array of object keys at a later point in the chain. This comes in handy when we're not exactly sure which keys are available and we only have a best guess. Let's try filtering by keys and values:

```
var object = {
    firstName: 'Jerald',
    lastName: 'Wolfe',
    age: 49
};

_(object)
    .keys()
    .filter(function(item) {
        return (/name$/i).test(item);
    })
    .thru(function(items) {
        return _.at(object, items);
    })
    .value();
// → [ "Jerald", "Wolfe" ]
```

The object we're wrapping has two property names that end in `name`. So we use the `keys()` function as the first step in the chain to grab all keys, and then we filter out the ones that don't end in `name`. Next, we use the `thru()` function to return the object property values that correspond to our key filter results. Similar actions can take place with object property values, especially when there's not much need to use keys. Let's look at an example of this:

```
var object = {
    first: 'Connie',
    last: 'Vargas',
    dob: new Date(1984, 08, 11)
};

_(object)
    .values()
    .filter(_.isDate)
    .map(function(item) {
        return item.toLocaleString();
    })
    .value();
// → [ "9/11/1984, 12:00:00 AM" ]
```

This chain grabs the property values of the wrapped object and filters out anything that's not a date. Then the `Date` objects found get mapped to an array of strings.

Omitting and picking properties

Picking certain object properties to use, as well as those to omit, has its uses in chains, especially when the wrapped value is a plain object and based on some criteria, there are certain properties we don't care to use. For example, we might have a collection that we want to transform into an indexed object, but along the way, we need to pick or omit values that should or shouldn't be there, respectively, as shown in the following example:

```
var collection = [
    { first: 'Tracey', last: 'Doyle', age: 40 },
    { first: 'Toby', last: 'Wright', age: 49 },
    { first: 'Leonard', last: 'Hunt', age: 32 },
    { first: 'Brooke', last: 'Briggs', age: 32 }
];

_(collection)
    .indexBy('last')
    .pick(function(value) {
        return value.age >= 35;
    })
    .transform(function(result, item, key) {
        result[key] = _.omit(item, 'last');
    })
    .value();
// →
// {
//   Doyle: { first: "Tracey", age: 40 },
//   Wright: { first: "Toby", age: 49 }
// }
```

This code indexes the array of objects by the `last` property value. The next step in the chain is to pick only items that have an `age` greater than `34`. Finally, since each item is indexed by the last name, we don't need the `last` property any more, so the `transform()` function uses `omit()` to get rid of it for each item, which is the last step in the chain.

Returning wrappers

Wrappers and the function call chains that follow don't exist randomly throughout our code. The next chapter covers this topic in more depth, so consider this as a teaser. So far, we've only looked at chains as they're constructed and executed in the same statement. However, if we're going through all the trouble of designing a call chain that serves a general purpose, wouldn't it be good not to keep assembling that chain? Let's design the chain with the following code:

```
function best(coll, prop, count) {
    return _(coll)
        .sortBy(prop)
        .takeRight(count);
}

var collection = [
    { name: 'Mathew', score: 92 },
    { name: 'Michele', score: 89 },
    { name: 'Joe', score: 74 },
    { name: 'Laurie', score: 83 }
];

var bestScore = best(collection, 'score', 2);

bestScore.value();
// →
// [
//   { name: "Michele", score": 89 },
//   { name: "Mathew", score: 92 }
// ]

bestScore.reverse().value();
// →
// [
//   { name: "Michele", score: 89 },
//   { name: "Mathew", score: 92 }
// ]

bestScore.pluck('name').value();
// → [ "Michele", "Mathew" ]
```

The `best()` function defined here returns a Lo-Dash wrapper instance. Notice that inside `best()`, we're actually chaining together function calls but none of them are actually called, which means that the return value of `best()` is a wrapper. This is illustrated by the `bestScrore` variable, which holds a wrapper instance. This wrapper can be called again and again without the need to reconstruct the function call chain. Nevertheless, if we need to tweak the chain slightly, we can build on it. We're doing this with `bestScore` by calling `reverse()` and `pluck()`.

Summary

This chapter introduced the concept of wrapped values and the function call chains applied to them. This versatile programming model, fundamental to Lo-Dash, assists in building complex chunks of functionality using compact and legible code. Chained calls aren't unique to Lo-Dash—they're popular in many other libraries, perhaps mostly so in jQuery.

Applications are faced with the tough job of filtering data—lots of data and lots of hard constraints. Instead of creating messy code with lots of temporary variables, we addressed several ways to construct complex filters using chains. After that, we looked at testing truth conditions using chains. These are like filters, except they don't return collection results but only truth statements expressed as Boolean values. We also looked at how to count items after they've moved through a function call chain.

Another fundamental practice we learned was transforming collections into alternative, more usable representations that better fit a given context. Like filtering, transforming collections is often better done using chains as it reduces the amount of code you have to write.

We closed the chapter with a look at how your functions can return wrappers that aren't necessarily executed immediately. This is the next step we take in building reusable Lo-Dash components, in the next chapter.

6
Application Building Blocks

The previous chapter addressed a key capability of Lo-Dash—wrapping values and executing chained function calls. One benefit of this style of coding is the ability to construct larger units of functionality that are generic and portable. We saw glimpses of both generality and portability when working with wrapper instances in the last chapter. The goal of this chapter is to implement these ideas. Writing an application is more than throwing together filters and maps that give you the data you need. Your code would grow messy in no time if you kept writing the same thing over and over again.

In this chapter, we'll learn how to write generic functions that internally utilize the Lo-Dash API. We'll also take chained function calls a step further by exploring the various ways they fit together, like puzzle pieces, and ultimately result in a robust foundation for your application. There comes a point when the functions you write for your application belong in the Lo-Dash infrastructure. That is, you need to mix your own generic code with the Lo-Dash API. We'll tackle that too.

In this chapter, we will cover the following topics:

- Generic functions
- Generic wrappers and chains
- Composing functions
- Creating mixins

Generic functions

Creating generic functions can make all the difference in the size and comprehensibility of our code. A generic function is useful in more than one context. It is loosely coupled to the application. That's what higher-level building blocks are all about; whether we're using a functional programming model, a more object-oriented approach, or a hybrid of the two, the key lies in generic components. As with most other aspects of programming, Lo-Dash provides many avenues to construct generic components. We'll address many of them throughout the course of this chapter. Let's start off by looking at functions that aren't so generic and how they compare with their more fluid cousins.

Specific functions

Whether a function is fit for one purpose or not, and whether it is fit for only one purpose, isn't always clear-cut. Depending on your perspective, there are degrees of specificity. Consider the following functions:

```
var collection = [
    { name: 'Ronnie', age: 43 },
    { name: 'Ben', age: 19 },
    { name: 'Sharon', age: 25 },
    { name: 'Melissa', age: 29 }
];

function collectionNames() {
    return _.map(collection, 'name');
}

function indirectionNames(coll, prop) {
    return _.map(coll, prop);
}

function genericCollNames(coll) {
    return _.map(coll, 'name');
}

function genericPropNames(prop) {
    return _.map(collection, prop);
}

collectionNames();
```

```
indirectionNames(collection, 'name');
genericCollNames(collection);

genericPropNames('name');
// → [ "Ronnie", "Ben", "Sharon", "Melissa" ]
```

Each of these four functions yields the same result, yet their implementations have their own unique consequences in our application. We can evaluate two generic properties of each function. First, we look at the collection that's being transformed—the main operand. Also, there are the secondary arguments passed in that affect the outcome.

The `collectionNames()` function is fairly specific, in that it expects a `collection` variable in its scope and hardcodes the `name` argument that is passed to `map()`. The `indirectionNames()` function is the opposite—it's completely generic because it accepts collection and property arguments, but it's also completely pointless since it's just a proxy and we might as well call `map()` directly. The `genericCollNames()` function is interesting; the collection we're mapping with this function is generic since it is passed as an argument, while the `name` argument is hardcoded. Lastly, the `genericPropNames()` function uses a generic argument when hardcoding the collection.

> Remember to consider each extreme—from indirection to fully hardcoding—when defining your functions. Either of these extremes is hardly worthwhile and the middle ground is somewhere to aim for. As for what you hardcode and what you keep generic, each has trade-offs that are unique to what you're building. You'll often find yourself changing these around as your application evolves.

Generic function arguments

JavaScript gives us some freedom in defining our functions. Not all arguments need to be statically declared ahead of time, as is the case in other languages. The `arguments` object is available to help us out, especially when we're trying to keep something generic. For example, certain callers may not pass all arguments. That's fine, our functions can cope and we can utilize this capability to define functions that are better equipped to generically interact with the Lo-Dash API, as shown in the following code:

```
function insert(coll, callback) {
    var toInsert;

    if (_.isFunction(callback)) {
```

```
            toInsert = _.slice(arguments, 2);
        } else {
            toInsert = _.slice(arguments, 1);
            callback = _.identity;
        }

        _.each(toInsert, function(item) {
            coll.splice(_.sortedIndex(coll, item, callback), 0, item);
        });

        return coll;

    }

    var collection = _.range(1, 11);

    insert(collection, 8.4);
    // → [ 1, 2, 3, 4, 5, 6, 7, 8, 8.4, 9, 10 ]

    insert(collection, 1.1, 6.9);
    // → [ 1, 1.1, 2, 3, 4, 5, 6, 6.9, 7, 8, 8.4, 9, 10 ]

    insert(collection, 4, 100);
    // → [ 1, 1.1, 2, 3, 4, 4, 5, 6, 6.9, 7, 8, 8.4, 9, 10, 100 ]
```

The `insert()` function accepts a `coll` and a `callback` argument. The collection is always required but the callback is optional. If no callback is provided, it defaults to the `identity()` function.

There's some additional trickery involved here as well, since any other arguments supplied to the function are the targets to be inserted into the collection. We use the `slice()` function to stick these in the `toInsert` variable and we slice them differently depending on whether or not a callback function was supplied. Then it's just a matter of iterating through each argument value to insert and passing our callback to `sortedIndex()`.

> Setting the callback value to `identity()` isn't strictly necessary here. That's the default behavior of most Lo-Dash functions that take callbacks. Being explicit doesn't hurt either, especially if we don't want the same default function.

Using partials

A handy pattern to solve the generic argument issues that arise is to use partials, that is, partially apply function arguments using the `partial()` function. This lets us build functions at runtime that can be used repeatedly, without having to always apply the same arguments. Sometimes it's not even feasible to provide function arguments. The following is an example of using partials:

```
var flattenProp = _.compose(_.flatten, _.prop),
    skills = _.partialRight(flattenProp, 'skills'),
    names = _.partialRight(flattenProp, 'name');

var collection = [
    { name: 'Danielle', skills: [ 'CSS', 'HTML', 'HTTP' ] },
    { name: 'Candice', skills: [ 'Lo-Dash', 'jQuery' ] },
    { name: 'Larry', skills: [ 'KineticJS', 'Jasmine' ] },
    { name: 'Norman', skills: [ 'Grunt', 'Require' ] }
];

_.contains(skills(collection), 'Lo-Dash');
// → true
_.contains(names(collection), 'Candice');
// → true
```

Our `flattenProp()` function is a composition of `flatten()` and `prop()`. The result that is returned is a flattened array. So, if any of these property values were themselves arrays, they just get added to the single array.

There's no need to always supply the name of the property we need flattened, especially when the data model used in our application shares many properties between entities. This is the perfect case for the use of partial functions. Remember, partials aren't entirely static—they do return functions after all. Our code defines two partial functions with the `prop` argument preapplied. Later on, we can use this function with specific collections.

> Creating partial functions out of generic functions is a form of function composition and a critical tool in building high-level application components.

Generic callbacks

It's one thing to design a function that's called manually in your code or in someone else's code. However, callbacks are essential to Lo-Dash. So it's always worthwhile to consider the fact that our functions are likely to be used as callbacks, as shown in the following code:

```
var YEAR_MILLISECONDS = 31560000000;

function validItem(item) {
    return item.age > 21 &&
        _.isString(item.first) &&
        _.isString(item.last);
}

function computed(item) {
    return _.extend({
        name: _.result(item, 'first', '') + ' ' +
            _.result(item, 'last', ''),
        yob: new Date(new Date() - (YEAR_MILLISECONDS * item.age))
            .getFullYear()
    }, item);
}

var invalidItem = _.negate(validItem);

    { first: 'Roderick', last: 'Campbell', age: 56 },
    { first: 'Monica', last: 'Salazar', age: 38 },
    { first: 'Ross', last: 'Andrews', age: 45 },
    { first: 'Martha', age: 51 }
];

_.every(collection, validItem);
// → false

_.filter(collection, validItem);
// →
// [
//   { first: "Roderick", last: "Campbell", age: 56 },
//   { first: "Monica", last: "Salazar", age: 38 },
//   { first: "Ross", last: "Andrews", age: 45 }
// ]

_.find(collection, invalidItem);
```

```
// → { first: "Martha", age: 51 }

_.map(collection, computed);
// →
// [
//   {
//     name: "Roderick Campbell",
//     yob: 1958,
//     first: "Roderick",
//     last: "Campbell",
//     age: 56
//   }, {
//     name: "Monica Salazar",
//     yob: 1976,
//     first: "Monica",
//     last: "Salazar",
//     age: 38
//   }, {
//     name: "Ross Andrews",
//     yob: 1969,
//     first: "Ross",
//     last: "Andrews",
//     age: 45
//   }, {
//     name: "Martha ",
//     yob: 1963,
//     first: "Martha",
//     age: 51 }]
```

Our first callback defined in this code is `validItem()`, and this is an incredibly useful function because there are bound to be lots of scenarios where you might be interested only in valid items. This function takes a generic `item` argument and returns `true` if that argument meets a certain criteria. This is the ideal format for callbacks that are iteratively applied to collections. The second callback is `computed()`, and this too takes a generic `item` argument. This callback is useful in mapping scenarios since it returns an extended version of the item, with computed properties. There's a third callback here too—`invalidItem()`. This is the inverse of the `validItem()` function and we're able to create it using `negate()`.

> You may have noticed that a lot of our callback functions use `item` as the first named argument. This is good practice as it gives the readers of your code a good indication that a given function is likely used as a callback somewhere.

Generic wrappers and chains

With generic functions under our belts, it's time to turn our attention to Lo-Dash wrapper instances and create generic function call chains. Chains are useful when you're stuck and you need a quick way out of a tricky programming situation, but they're also useful in the generic sense. That is, you can compose chains of functionality that are general enough to apply in a variety of contexts.

Generic filters

Let's start by taking a look at generic filters and how they can be utilized in our functions. Filters are especially suitable for chained function calls since they can be stitched together by applying a filter after a preceding filter. There are often some kinds of sorting or other constraints that take place at the end of a filter, such as limiting the number of results returned, as shown in the following code:

```
function byName(coll, name, take) {
    return _(coll)
        .filter({ name: name })
        .take(_.isUndefined(take) ? 100 : take)
        .value();
}

var collection = [
    { name: 'Theodore', enabled: true },
    { name: 'Leslie', enabled: true },
    { name: 'Justin', enabled: false },
    { name: 'Leslie', enabled: false }
];

byName(collection, 'Leslie');
// →
// [
//   { name: "Leslie", enabled: true },
//   { name: "Leslie", enabled: false }
// ]

byName(_.filter(collection, 'enabled'), 'Leslie');
// →
// [ { name: "Leslie", enabled: true } ]

byName(_(collection).filter('enabled'), 'Leslie');
// →
// [ { name: "Leslie", enabled": true } ]
```

Our `byName()` function wraps the passed-in collection and applies a `filter()` and a `take()` operation. It also accepts a couple of arguments. The `name` argument is the name we're filtering the collection on. The `take` argument is optional, and if supplied, specifies the number of items to return. If the `take` argument is missing, we default to `100`.

There are three different invocations of `byName()` demonstrated in the preceding code. The first invocation is the most straightforward. We're simply passing the name, `Leslie`, since this is the name we want to filter the collection by. The next invocation performs a `filter()` operation on the collection, then passes its result to `byName()`. The last invocation gets the same result as the second. However, you'll notice that we've already wrapped the collection, and since the `filter()` function is **chainable**, the wrapper instance gets passed as the `coll` argument.

> Rewrapping a Lo-Dash wrapper is safe. The constructor recognizes this and knows how to handle it.

This function constructs a somewhat generic chain. We can pass in the collection at runtime along with the name value we would like to filter by. We can even pass the number of results we'd like to take, and the function doesn't care if it gets a wrapped value. This latter point is especially useful since it allows us to use other functions we've developed that perform chained function calls, return these chains, and use them. The limiting factor of `byName()` is that it calls `value()`, and returns the unwrapped collection.

Returning chains

It's almost always a good idea to have our functions that construct wrappers return those same wrapper instances. In the previous section, our function unwrapped the value after the call chain had completed and returned it. The problem with this approach is that the caller may have more operations to apply on the chain. To do this, the value would need to be wrapped again. Lo-Dash wrapper instances should have the freedom to move about your code and be passed around from function to function, as if it were a plain array, as in the following example:

```
function sort(coll, prop, desc) {
    var wrapper = _(coll).sortBy(prop);
    return desc ? wrapper.reverse() : wrapper;
}

var collection = [
    { first: 'Bobby', last: 'Pope' },
    { first: 'Debbie', last: 'Reid' },
```

```
        { first: 'Julian', last: 'Garcia' },
        { first: 'Jody', last: 'Greer' }
    ];

    sort(collection, 'first').value(),
    // →
    // [
    //   { first: "Bobby", last: "Pope" },
    //   { first: "Debbie", last: "Reid" },
    //   { first: "Jody", last: "Greer" },
    //   { first: "Julian", last: "Garcia" }
    // ]

    sort(collection, 'first', true).value(),
    // →
    // [
    //   { first: "Julian", last: "Garcia" },
    //   { first: "Jody", last: "Greer" },
    //   { first: "Debbie", last: "Reid" },
    //   { first: "Bobby", last: "Pope" }
    // ]

    sort(collection, 'last')
        .takeRight(2)
        .pluck('last')
        .value();
    // → [ "Pope", "Reid" ]
```

The `sort()` function is quite straightforward and doesn't seem to do all that much. On the face of it, it just takes in a collection, sorts it, and returns it. Yes, that's the goal at a high level. First, you'll notice that the `coll` argument is wrapped in the Lo-Dash constructor function—the argument value can be either a wrapper instance or an unwrapped value. The function also accepts a property name or a function callback to sort the collection by. The `desc` argument is optional and it reverses the sort order if `true`.

The major difference between this function and the `byName()` function we implemented earlier is that `sort()` will always return a wrapper instance. This means that we don't have to rewrap the returned value, should the caller need to add more function calls to the chain. You can see this in action with the last invocation of `sort()` in the preceding code. Here we're adding a `takeRight()` and a `pluck()` call to the chain. Designing functions in this way gives us great flexibility in how we're able to use wrappers throughout our code. The general rule would be to let your functions be wrapper friendly, both in what they accept as arguments and in what they return.

The trade-off, it would appear, is that the caller needs to call not only your function, but also the `value()` function. Sometimes, this can be a pain if all you want is the actual value so that you can start working with it, but remember that the chain itself isn't executed until the `value()` function is called. This has implications for lazy evaluation, which simply means that the return values aren't computed until `value()` is called. So this could actually be a desired trait—the ability to build chains without executing them.

> You should always document in one form or another that your function does indeed return a Lo-Dash wrapper and that the caller needs to call `value()`.

Composing functions

Whether our functions are called manually, used as a callback by another function, or used in some other context that involves chains, function composition helps construct larger pieces of functionality. For example, we may have two smaller functions that serve niche purposes on their own. When we're in scenarios where these functions may come in handy, we can use the functional tools in Lo-Dash to compose a new function that utilizes them, rather than roll out our own.

Composing generic functions

Earlier in the chapter, we emphasized the idea that functions need to be generic if they're to be of any service in more than one context. The same idea holds true when composing larger components of smaller functions. The smaller functions need to be generic if we're going to use them to compose anything larger. Likewise, the composite should also be as generic as possible so that we can use it as an ingredient in a larger piece of the application. This is shown in the following code:

```
function enabledIndex(obj) {
    return _.transform(obj, function(result, value, key) {
        result[key] = _.result(value, 'enabled', false);
    });
}

var collection = [
    { name: 'Claire', enabled: true },
    { name: 'Patricia', enabled: false },
    { name: 'Mario', enabled: true },
```

```
        { name: 'Jerome', enabled: false }
    ];

    var indexByName = _.partialRight(_.indexBy, 'name'),
        enabled = _.partial(_.flow(indexByName, enabledIndex),
        collection);

    enabled();
    // →
    // {
    //   Claire: true,
    //   Patricia: false,
    //   Mario: true,
    //   Jerome: false
    // }

    collection.push({ name: 'Gloria', enabled: true });
    enabled();
    // →
    // {
    //   Claire: true,
    //   Patricia: false,
    //   Mario: true,
    //   Jerome: false,
    //   Gloria: true
    // }
```

This code has two generic utility functions. The `indexByName()` function takes a collection and returns an object where the keys are the `name` property for every item in the collection. The `enabledIndex()` function takes an object and converts each property value to a Boolean value, based on its `enabled` property. Perhaps, each of these functions is used on its own elsewhere in your application, but now, while developing a new component, we've come up with a use case that warrants using them together.

Rather than having to call each function independently and feed the output of the first function to the second, we decide to compose an `enabled()` function. This way, we can use a simple invocation any time we need the object structure that maps the name to the `enabled` Boolean value. This is done by partially applying the collection argument to the function we're creating, using `flow()`. The `flow()` function passes the first argument to the first function, and the next, and so on, returning the result.

> This code makes the assumption that the `name` property is unique for each object. Otherwise, it wouldn't be worth indexing like this.

Composing callbacks

The `enabled()` function we just composed in the preceding section was intended to be directly called by our code somewhere. Callbacks, on the other hand, are generally passed to a Lo-Dash function. Passing inline anonymous functions works fine, except when you find yourself writing the same callback functions over and over again, or at least, similar functions with little variance. There's no reason that our application can't compose generic callbacks and make them available throughout the application to encourage reuse over duplication. Let's take a look at this example:

```
var collection = [
    { first: 'Andrea', last: 'Stewart', age: 28 },
    { first: 'Clarence', last: 'Johnston', age: 31 },
    { first: 'Derek', last: 'Lynch', age: 37 },
    { first: 'Susan', last: 'Rodgers', age: 41 }
];

var minimal = _.flow(_.identity,
    _.partialRight(_.pick, [ 'last', 'age' ]));

_.map(collection, minimal);
// →
// [
//   { last: "Stewart", age: 28 },
//   { last: "Johnston", age: 31 },
//   { last: "Lynch", age: 37 },
//   { last: "Rodgers", age: 41 }
// ]
```

A common problem faced by callback functions is that they have no control over how they're invoked. One function may invoke each of its callbacks using a single argument, while the next uses three arguments. This prevents us from doing certain things we'd otherwise like to, such as composing callbacks using Lo-Dash functions that are already built and ready to go.

The `minimal()` function defined in this code is used to pick only the essential object properties from the passed-in argument. Let's say we want to pass this callback to `map()`. Well, `map()` invokes its callbacks with three arguments, the first one being the actual item we're interested in. This means that it's nearly impossible for us to use Lo-Dash functions with partially applied arguments as callbacks.

The workaround we've employed with the `minimal()` callback is to use `flow()` to compose the callback. You'll notice that the first function is `identity()`. This does nothing more than returning whatever value is passed to it. So in other words, it returns the first argument. Next in the flow is our partial function that uses `pick()`. And guess what? It'll only get one argument passed to it, as we need, even if used in a `map()` callback, which is called with three arguments.

Composing chains

Now we'll look at composing functions that work with chains. As we've seen throughout this chapter, it's beneficial for you and anyone else who uses your functions to be flexible in what your functions accept as arguments, and what they return. For example, a function that accepts a wrapper and returns a wrapper means that it can be passed just about anything and that the caller is free to extend the call chain. Just as we can compose plain functions and callback functions, we can also compose functions whose main focus is working with chains. Take a look at the following example:

```
function sorted(wrapper) {
    return _(wrapper).sortBy();
}

function rejectOdd(wrapper) {
    return _(wrapper).reject(function(item) {
        return item % 2
    });
}

var sortedEvens = _.flow(sorted, rejectOdd),
    evensSorted = _.flow(rejectOdd, sorted,
        _.partialRight(_.result, 'value')),
    collection = _.shuffle(_.range(1, 11));

sortedEvens(collection)
    .reverse()
    .value();
```

```
// → [ 10, 8, 6, 4, 2 ]

evensSorted(collection);
// → [ 2, 4, 6, 8, 10 ]
```

The `rejectOdd()` function here takes either a collection or a wrapper instance as the first argument and filters out the odd numbers. Notice that it returns a wrapper instead of the unwrapped value. We use this wrapper-friendly function to compose two new functions. The first is `sortedEvens()`, which uses our `sorted()` function to sort the collection. This returns a wrapper instance, which is then fed to the `rejectOdd()` function. The `evensSorted()` function does something similar but in a different order. It rejects the odd numbers before sorting them, and then it uses `partialRight()` to unwrap the value using `result()`.

You can see that when we call the `sortedEvens()` function, it returns a wrapper instance because we're extending the function call chain with `reverse()`, and then we get the value. However, we don't perform this extension with our composed `evensSorted()` function because it unwraps the value for us.

Method composition

Sometimes, it makes sense to attach functions to a specific object scope or implement methods. If the function requires instance-specific values in order to operate, then it's probably a good idea to implement the function as a property of the prototype so that it is always available to instances. So we can use the techniques we've looked at so far in this chapter to assist us with building object methods, which are yet another building block in our application's structure. Take a look at the following example of object methods:

```
function validThru(next, value) {
    return value && next;
}

function User(first, last, age) {
    this.first = first;
    this.last = last;
    this.age = age;
}

User.prototype.valid = function() {
    return _.chain(this.first)
        .isString()
```

```
            .thru(_.partial(validThru, this.last))
            .isString()
            .thru(_.partial(validThru, this.age))
            .isFinite()
            .value();
    }

    new User('Orlando', 'Olson', 25).valid();
    // → true

    new User('Timothy', 'Davis').valid();
    // → false

    new User('Colleen').valid();
    // → false
```

Our `User` constructor accepts three arguments, and all of these are set as instance values. We've also implemented a `valid()` method. We're utilizing a function call chain here to validate each of the instance attributes. Note that we've enabled explicit chaining here. This means the functions in the chain that would normally return unwrapped values, won't. We're doing this because we need to pass primitive values through the chain.

The `first` property is wrapped, and we validate that it is a string using the `isString()` function. Next, we use `thru()`. We're using our `validThru()` function here as a callback to `thru()`. Basically, if the value returned by `isString()`, the previous call, is `true`, then return the next value. In this case, it's partially applied as the `last` property. The same steps are performed with the `age` property.

What's nice about this approach is that the chain requires access to several properties and all enclosed within the method. We can then construct a readable chain that validates all of these properties and doesn't require several control flow statements, which can be more difficult to maintain than two lines in a chain.

Creating mixins

The last major building block we'll visit in this chapter is the mixin. Lo-Dash has a `mixin()` function that lets us extend the API by providing our own functions. There are two reasons you'd want to do such a thing. The first is that by placing your generic toolset in the Lo-Dash object, you can have access to them wherever the _ symbol is accessible. The second reason is that once you've mixed in your own function, it can be used as a piece in a function call chain.

Creating an average() function

There's only so many utilities a library such as Lo-Dash can feasibly ship. The ones that are viewed as most applicable to common users are the ones we get out of the box. This doesn't mean that the application you're working on doesn't have a high-value use case you wish Lo-Dash implemented. For example, assume your application computes averages all over the place. While the library doesn't ship with an `average` function, that doesn't mean we can't add this function to the code:

```
_.mixin({average: function(coll, callback) {
    return _(coll)
        .map(callback)
        .reduce(function(result, item) {
            return result + item;
        }) / _.size(coll);
}});

var collection = [
    { name: 'Frederick', age: 41, enabled: true },
    { name: 'Jasmine', age: 29, enabled: true },
    { name: 'Virgil', age: 47, enabled: true },
    { name: 'Lila', age: 22, enabled: false }
];

_.average(collection, 'age');
// → 34.75

_.average(collection, function(item) {
    return _.size(item.name);
});
// → 6.5

_(collection)
    .filter('enabled')
    .average('age');
// → 39
```

The computation that takes place in our `average()` mixin is really straightforward—division of the items by the length of the collection. It's the mapping of these items we need to consider. If you look at the arguments accepted by the `average()` mixin, you'll notice that it takes a collection, which is always required, and a callback. The callback is optional and can be anything that's accepted as a `map()` callback. Our chain then reduces these items to a sum before they're divided by the collection size.

You can see that the average() function is now part of the Lo-Dash object and that we're able to pass a string argument or a function callback. You can also see that the function is chainable, as demonstrated in the last invocation.

Creating a distance() function

Let's create a more involved mixin function called distance. It'll use the Levenshtein distance algorithm to measure the edit distance between two strings. We'll create another mixin that uses distance(). This function will sort collections by the shortest distance from the target string:

```
_.mixin({distance: function(source, target) {
    var sourceSize = _.size(source),
        targetSize = _.size(target),
        matrix;

    if (sourceSize === 0) {
        return targetSize;
    }
    if (targetSize === 0) {
        return sourceSize;
    }

    matrix = _.map(_.range(targetSize + 1), function(item) {
        return [ item ];
    });

     _.each(_.range(sourceSize + 1), function(item) {
        matrix[0][item] = item;
    });

    _.each(target, function(targetItem, targetIndex) {
        _.each(source, function(sourceItem, sourceIndex) {
            if (targetItem === sourceItem) {
                matrix[targetIndex + 1][sourceIndex + 1] =
                    matrix[targetIndex][sourceIndex];
            } else {
                matrix[targetIndex + 1][sourceIndex + 1] = Math.min(
                    matrix[targetIndex][sourceIndex] + 1,
                    Math.min(matrix[targetIndex + 1][sourceIndex] + 1,
                        matrix[targetIndex][sourceIndex + 1] + 1));
            }
        });
```

```
        });

        return matrix[targetSize][sourceSize]

    }});

    _.mixin({closest: function(coll, value, callback) {
        return _.sortBy(coll, _.flow(_.callback(callback), function(item)
    {
            return _.distance(value, item);
        }));
    }});

    var collection = [
        'console',
        'compete',
        'competition',
        'compose',
        'composition'
    ];

    _.distance('good', 'food');
    // → 1

    _.closest(collection, 'composite');
    // →
    // [
    //   "compose",
    //   "compete",
    //   "composition",
    //   "console",
    //   "competition"
    // ]

    _(collection)
        .closest('consulate')
        .first();
    // → "console"
```

We won't fixate on the details of the Levenshtein distance algorithm; there are plenty of online resources available for that. The `distance()` mixin we just implemented accepts a `source` string and a `target` string with which to compare it. The return value represents the number of edits needed to make the target match the source. For example, the call to `distance()` in the preceding code yields `1`.

The `closest()` mixin function uses `distance()` as a `sortBy()` callback. This is a useful function because it's often a collection of the target strings we're comparing the source string to. Further, since it's a mixin function, we're able to use it in a chain. The last call to `closest()` does this and then uses `first()` to grab the closest value.

Summary

In this chapter, we learned some useful approaches to building higher-level application components. Functions are the fundamental unit of Lo-Dash programming, so it's important that we properly utilize all that they have to offer. We addressed some common issues faced when thinking about how to design reusable functions. For example, the specificity of a function and the arguments it accepts can impact where and how the function can be used in your Lo-Dash code.

Generic wrappers and the chained function calls they implement are powerful tools, and there are many implementation options that come with them. We walked through several examples of how different aspects of chains work, and how these wrappers interact with the various functions in our application.

Function composition is an essential part of functional programming and we learned how to exploit the functional tools Lo-Dash provides to compose larger pieces of our application code. These include the generic functions we call manually, and callback functions. This chapter closed with a look at the mixin functions that are used to extend the Lo-Dash API. The next chapter will show you how to take these application-level Lo-Dash components, and make sure they play nicely alongside other libraries.

7 Using Lo-Dash with Other Libraries

The previous chapter showed us what our Lo-Dash code starts to look like as it falls in place within a larger application. Things get factored into a more generic, reusable form, and they're named and structured consistently. Patterns start to emerge, and as your code starts to realize these patterns, it takes the shape of a production-ready system.

In the spirit of deploying Lo-Dash code to a production environment, this chapter addresses the ecosystem into which our code is tossed when deemed stable. Lo-Dash does a lot, but there are some tasks that this library is simply not well suited for. In other words, it's highly unlikely that Lo-Dash is the only library your application will use.

The best way to keep our code organized and modular is by using modules. Module technology has gained a lot of attention over the last few years in the JavaScript community, and Lo-Dash is no exception. We can make it work using the same module loaders that applications use. There are also Lo-Dash packages available for Node.js.

In this chapter, we will cover the following topics:

- Modules
- jQuery
- Backbone
- Node.js

Modules

If you've done any frontend development in the past few years, you have probably heard of AMD modules, if you haven't already experimented with them. AMD is growing fast, with no shortage of production deployments around the world. This modular movement in frontend development stemmed from a lack of a decent way to organize large-scale projects that have many dependencies. Before modules for the web were a thing, the only tool at our disposal for organizing dependencies was the <script> element. This is still an accepted way to pull in JavaScript code—except when there are hundreds of modules.

Modularity, especially frontend web development modularity, is a large topic —too large for this book (let alone for this chapter) to properly address. So let's strip the topic down to the relevant parts for us, the Lo-Dash programmers. It's good programming practice to divide our code into modules that serve a single purpose. This provides a good separation of concerns and allows our components to evolve more easily and independently of one another.

In this section, we'll take a look at **RequireJS**, one of the leading AMD module loader technologies available. Lo-Dash has builds that help us utilize this technology and construct modules of our own. With that said, let's get into some of the practical nitty-gritty.

> **AMD** stands for **asynchronous module definition**, a simple pattern followed by many JavaScript components. It's not a recognized specification, although something is brewing in the upcoming ES6 specification. There's a related pattern called UMD, which aims to be more universal than AMD and has some questionable fallback modes. My advice is to stick to something that's easy to use, such as RequireJS, until there's an adopted standard that's widely supported.

Organizing your code with modules

Let's see what a basic module looks like. The idea is that a definition function returns the component that the module defines. The component could be a function, an object, a string, or any value for that matter. If you're developing a Lo-Dash application, your modules are likely to return functions.

> Since RequireJS makes XHR requests, it's a lot easier to serve your JavaScript modules with a simple static web server. The code that is shipped with this book has a `Gruntfile`, which lets you run a simple web server. However, you'll need Node.js installed. There are plenty of resources all over the Internet that can be used to install Node on any platform. Once Node is available, you can install Grunt with the following command:
>
> `npm install -g grunt-cli grunt-contrib-connect`
>
> This will make the `grunt` command available on your system. From within the root code directory, where the `Gruntfile.js` file is located, run the following command:
>
> `grunt connect`
>
> You'll see some output about the server running forever. Pressing *Ctrl* + *C* will stop it. And that's it! You can navigate to `http://0.0.0.0:8000/chapter7.html` to run the examples from this chapter.

Consider the following code:

```
define([], function() {
    return function(coll, filter) {
        return _(coll)
            .filter(filter)
            .reduce(function(result, item) {
                return result + item.age;
            }, 0) / _.size(coll);
    };
});
```

You can see that the `define()` function takes two arguments. The first is an array of modules that we're dependent on and the second is a function that returns the component this module defines. In this case, our module doesn't have any external dependencies and it returns an anonymous function. This function takes a `coll` and a `filter` argument. Then we use the Lo-Dash constructor to wrap the collection and we reduce it to the average value. Next, let's take a look at how this module gets used:

```
var collection = [
    { name: 'Frederick', age: 37 },
    { name: 'Tasha', age: 45 },
    { name: 'Lisa', age: 33 },
    { name: 'Michael', age: 41 }
];

require([ 'modules/average-age' ], function(averageAge) {
```

```
        averageAge(collection);
        // → 39
    });
```

You can see here that our call to the `require()` function passes an array of module dependencies. In this case, we're dependent on the `average-age` module. The function callback is triggered when this module is loaded, evaluated, and ready to use. The `averageAge` argument is the value returned by the module. In this case, it's the function we defined earlier, and we show how it can be applied to a collection.

Requiring Lo-Dash

The downside to our `average-age` module is that it doesn't define any explicit dependencies. Yet, it clearly depends on Lo-Dash being available. So how does this code even work? Where does the _ variable get defined? Well, the only reason the preceding example runs is because we've included Lo-Dash on the page using the standard `<script>` tag. This adds the _ symbol to the global namespace.

This goes against one of the grounding principles of modules—there shouldn't be a need for global variables. What we end up with are implicit dependencies, as is the case in the previous code. This means our modules that use this implicit dependency aren't as portable as they could be. If that `<script>` tag goes away, our module stops working. Thankfully, we can define our modules that depend on Lo-Dash as having this dependency explicitly, as shown in the following code:

```
define([ 'lodash' ], function(_) {
    return function(coll) {
        return _(coll)
            .sortBy(function(item) {
                return item.first + '' + item.last;
            });
    };
});
```

Here, you can see that instead of passing an empty array as the first argument to `define()`, we have a string that points to the Lo-Dash module. Now the _ symbol is an argument within our `define()` function instead of being referenced globally. Let's see this module being put to use now:

```
var collection = [
    { first: 'Georgia', last: 'Todd' },
    { first: 'Andrea', last: 'Gretchen' },
    { first: 'Ruben', last: 'Green' },
```

```
    { first: 'Johnny', last: 'Tucker' }
];

require([ 'modules/sort-name' ], function(sortName) {
    sortName(collection).value();
    // →
    // [
    //   { first: "Andrea", last: "Gretchen" },
    //   { first: "Georgia", last: "Todd" },
    //   { first: "Johnny", last: "Tucker" },
    //   { first: "Ruben", last: "Green" }
    // ]
});
```

Here, we require our `sort-name` module as a dependency and the `sortName()` function is an argument to the `require()` callback function. The function sorts an input collection by name and returns a wrapper instance. This is illustrated here, by calling `sortBy()` followed by `value()`. This is actually a good thing because it means that the returned wrapper instance can be extended before it is evaluated and unwrapped.

You'll also notice that we're indirectly depending on Lo-Dash here because we depend on `sort-name`. We can call the `value()` function and extend the returned wrapper without an explicit reference to the _ symbol. This means that, should the `sort-name` module no longer rely on Lo-Dash at some point in the future, our function will still work, although we might have to remove the `value()` invocation.

There's another step involved with getting Lo-Dash to work with RequireJS. Let's take a look at the `main.js` configuration file that helps RequireJS figure out where to find modules and what they expose:

```
require.config({
    paths: {
        lodash: 'lib/lodash'
    },
    shim: {
        lodash: { exports: '_' }
    }
});
```

Our code referenced `lodash` as a dependency. This path configuration tells RequireJS where to find that module. The `shim` configuration section is for modules that aren't defined as AMD modules. Since this is the case with Lo-Dash, we have to add a shim that tells RequireJS what's actually returned when something requires the concerned module.

Working with Lo-Dash AMD modules

It turns out that there's a better way to use Lo-Dash in the form of AMD modules. Lo-Dash has specific AMD builds available for download and these don't require a shim. Another benefit of obtaining Lo-Dash components this way is that we don't have to pull down the entire library if we depend on only a handful of functions. For example, let's see how we can depend on function categories:

```
function Person(first, last) {
    this.first = first;
    this.last = last;
}

Person.prototype.name = function() {
    return this.first + '' + this.last;
}

var collection = [
    new Person('Douglas', 'Wright'),
    new Person('Tracy', 'Wilson'),
    new Person('Ken', 'Phelps'),
    new Person('Meredith', 'Simmons')
];

require([ 'lib/lodash-amd/collection' ], function(_) {
    _.invoke(collection, 'name');
    // →
    // [
    //    "Douglas Wright",
    //    "Tracy Wilson",
    //    "Ken Phelps",
    //    "Meredith Simmons"
    // ]
});
```

We're using the AMD build of Lo-Dash in this example. This is made apparent by the module path that we require. The `collection` module is defined as an AMD module and contains all the collection-related functions. You can see that we're using the _ symbol as the function argument. This means the code that uses the collection functions can be written just as if it is using any Lo-Dash module. For instance, if we were to require the full Lo-Dash API instead of just the collection functions, none of the code would need to change. Instead, we're only requiring a subset of Lo-Dash, thus saving the network delivery cost.

The code is using the `invoke()` function on our collection to call the `name()` method on each item while collecting the results. However, that's only one function. There's still a lot in the collections category that we require and are not using at all. Let's see how we can use more fine-grained Lo-Dash function dependencies:

```
var collection = [
    { name: 'Susan', age: 57, enabled: false },
    { name: 'Marcus', age: 45, enabled: true },
    { name: 'Ray', age: 25, enabled: false },
    { name: 'Dora', age: 19, enabled: true }
];

require([
    'lib/lodash-amd/collection/filter',
    'lib/lodash-amd/function/partial'
], function(filter, partial) {
    function valid(age, item) {
        return item.enabled && item.age >= age;
    }

    filter(collection, partial(valid, 25));
    // → [ { age: 45, enabled: true, name: "Marcus" } ]

});
```

As you can see when you drill into the categories, there's a specific module for any given function you'd like to include. The preceding code is using two Lo-Dash functions. The `filter()` function comes from the collection category and the `partial()` function comes from the function category. Both functions are passed directly as callback arguments. Since both of these function modules are themselves defined as AMD modules, they require only the internal dependencies needed to work. This means that we're only requiring what we need, which might only be one or two functions in certain contexts, such as our preceding example.

The downside to this level of granularity is that if you're unsure of what you need, you'll constantly have to modify your list of model dependencies. Lo-Dash has a lot to offer, and it's a good idea to utilize Lo-Dash functions wherever you can. For example, if you're wrapping values and chaining together function calls, it's tough to know in advance which functions you're going to require. So it's probably a good idea to obtain the whole API so that there's no possibility of something you want to use not being there. Consider the following code:

```
var collection = [
    { name: 'Allan', age: 29, enabled: false },
```

```
        { name: 'Edward', age: 43, enabled: false },
        { name: 'Evelyn', age: 39, enabled: true },
        { name: 'Denise', age: 34, enabled: true }
    ];

    require([ 'lib/lodash-amd/main' ], function(_) {
        _(collection)
            .filter('enabled')
            .sortBy('age')
            .reverse()
            .map('name')
            .value();
        // → [ "Evelyn", "Denise" ]
    });
```

This is similar to our first example, where we required the entire Lo-Dash API. The difference here is that this is the AMD build, so we require the `main` Lo-Dash module, which includes everything we'll need. The other difference is that with this approach, there's no need to set up paths or shims within the main RequireJS configuration file.

jQuery

jQuery is undoubtedly one of the most successful and widely used technologies of all time. And it came into being because of browser inconsistencies; John Resig decided to do something about it. Rather than having the application developers maintain their own code that deals with all the mundane cross-browser issues, why not let jQuery handle that stuff for them?

jQuery has evolved over the years, thanks to thousands and thousands of users and contributing developers wanting to make frontend development less intimidating. Over time, it has changed certain aspects of itself and added new features to keep up with the changing environments in which it resides.

It's safe to say that jQuery has changed the way frontend development is done and will continue to do so because of its mass adoption. Several web standards that exist today are rooted in jQuery. Lo-Dash is similar to jQuery in a lot of ways. While it's not nearly as mature as jQuery, it's being rapidly adopted. Like jQuery, Lo-Dash originated from an effort to fix cross-browser issues and performance issues present in Underscore.js. The development effort of Lo-Dash has expanded much beyond a simple drop-in replacement for Underscore.js and will certainly influence future JavaScript specifications.

So jQuery and Lo-Dash are similar in their effectiveness. Where they differ is in the specific problems they solve for programmers. Let's take a closer look at those and see whether there is a way in which the two libraries can complement one another.

Challenges faced by Lo-Dash

Lo-Dash is a low-level framework that augments JavaScript at the language level. Low-level is a relative term. It's not that Lo-Dash doesn't have any abstractions; it has plenty. It's just that there's a lot more to frontend development than just JavaScript. Lo-Dash isn't good at any of those other things, nor is it intended to be.

While you can use Lo-Dash to write better code, that's only half the battle. Standalone JavaScript code doesn't get you very far. If you're developing an application, at some point, you're going to eventually touch the DOM. You're going to make API calls that load your application data and change the state of the server-side resources. You're also going to deal with the asynchronous nature of these calls and user events, while taking care to perform well and prevent leaks.

Frontend development is a complicated endeavor but Lo-Dash is great for all things in JavaScript. Writing concise, readable code that performs well is where Lo-Dash shines. This generally means the core of your frontend code. For everything else, there are other libraries, such as jQuery.

Challenges faced by jQuery

One of the reasons jQuery is so attractive to programmers is its low barrier to entry. Anyone building a website can immediately learn and benefit from jQuery, often in a day or two. At the same time, it's powerful enough to scale from a basic site to a powerful web application. DOM traversal and manipulation are one thing jQuery excels at, but it's also capable of dealing with complicated Ajax calls, DOM events, and asynchronous callbacks.

These are all the areas Lo-Dash lacks any support in. Again, this is intentional. The two libraries serve different purposes. However, they're also complementary and often sit side by side in the same application, carrying out their roles. What jQuery doesn't have is a set of tools to aid the programmer inside all of these callback functions that run in response to Ajax requests, user events, and so on. This is not what it's meant for. You're free to use any library you like to enhance the core application business logic, and Lo-Dash is one such choice.

The focused nature of both Lo-Dash and jQuery leaves us with a clear separation of concerns. jQuery lets the Lo-Dash programmer worry about creating high-quality functional code. We've already seen how to utilize RequireJS with Lo-Dash in an effort to produce modular components. Let's now look at how we can use Lo-Dash alongside jQuery.

Using jQuery instances as collections

Perhaps, the most common use case of jQuery is querying the DOM for elements. The result is a jQuery object that closely resembles an array. We can exercise our Lo-Dash know-how to treat these instances as collections. For example, let's compare the jQuery `map()` function to the Lo-Dash `map()` function:

```
var i = 1000;
console.time('$');
while (i--) {
    $('li').map(function() {
        return $(this).html();
    });
}
console.timeEnd('$');
i = 1000;
console.time('_');
while (i--) {
    _.map($('li'), function(item) {
        return $(item).html();
    });
}
console.timeEnd('_');
// →
// $: 64.127ms
// _: 27.434ms
```

The mapped output of both approaches is exactly the same. Even the code differences are subtle at best. The difference is only in the looping performance—the Lo-Dash `map()` function will always have an edge over the jQuery `map()` function due to the differences in implementation.

> The following chapter goes into greater detail on why iterative Lo-Dash functions perform the way they do.

The performance gain isn't all that great. What's a few milliseconds here and there? The preceding example only finds a handful of elements, and the test is repeated 1,000 times. In production, you're probably going to be dealing with larger query results, iterated more than 1,000 times, and over time, the milliseconds start to add up.

Is there anything fundamentally wrong with the performance of jQuery `map()`? Absolutely not. If it works, use it. This change itself isn't going to pleasantly surprise your users. On the other hand, if you're a Lo-Dash programmer, you're going to use it for what it's good at. Lo-Dash is very good at iterating over collections. jQuery is very good at querying the DOM, and it still takes up this responsibility. So what's the code cost of implementing this improvement? Essentially zero.

Binding functions

In the previous section, we looked at an area where Lo-Dash and jQuery overlap. We chose the Lo-Dash approach because it made sense to do so, both from a responsibility perspective (iterating over collections) and a cost-to-implement perspective (the code looks nearly identical). Another area of overlap is function binding. jQuery has tools available to bind functions to a given context, but Lo-Dash has better functional tools. Let's compare the two approaches again:

```
function boundFunction(result, item) {
    return result + this.multiplier * item;
}

var scope = { multiplier: 10 },
    collection = _.range(1, 1000),
    jQueryBound = $.proxy(boundFunction, scope),
    lodashBound = _.bind(boundFunction, scope);

console.time('$');
console.log(_.reduce(collection, jQueryBound));
console.timeEnd('$');

console.time('_');
console.log(_.reduce(collection, lodashBound));
console.timeEnd('_');
// →
// 4994991
// $: 3.214ms
// 4994991
// _: 0.567ms
```

Both approaches reduce the collection to the same result. The code is basically identical; the only difference is the way the callback passed to `reduce()` is bound. The context we're binding the functions to is a plain object with a `multiplier` property that's looked up when the callback is run. It's looked up by referencing `this`, which is why we have to bind the context before passing the callback to the `reduce()` function.

The first approach uses the `proxy()` jQuery function while the second approach uses the Lo-Dash `bind()` function. As with the preceding example of `map()`, the performance edge goes to Lo-Dash, there's no cost to implement it, and it's something that Lo-Dash was designed to do well. So if you're passing callbacks to jQuery event functions, `bind()` is just as viable as `proxy()` and is within the scope of something Lo-Dash is good at.

Working with jQuery deferred instances

We've seen how Lo-Dash can aid in iterating over DOM elements after they've been queried by jQuery. We've also seen how Lo-Dash can improve function bindings in our jQuery code. Let's turn things around and see where jQuery can help our Lo-Dash code:

```
function query(coll, filter, sort) {
    var deferred = $.Deferred(),
        _coll = _(coll).filter(filter);

    if (sort) {
        _coll.sortBy(_.isBoolean(sort) ? undefined : sort);
    }

    if (_.size(coll) > 5000) {
        _.defer(function() {
            deferred.resolve(_coll.value());
        });
    } else {
       deferred.resolve(_coll.value());
    }

    return deferred.promise();
}

var collection = _.map(_.range(_.random(10000)), function(item) {
    return {
```

```
            id: item,
            enabled: !!_.random()
        };
    }), resultSize;

    console.log('Collection size: ' + _.size(collection));
    query(collection, 'enabled', true).done(function(result) {
        resultSize = _.size(result);
        console.log('Result size: ' + resultSize);
    });

    if (!resultSize) {
        console.log('Awaiting results...');
    }
    // →
    // Collection size: 9071
    // Awaiting results...
    // Result size: 4635
```

Here we're utilizing the `Deferred` jQuery object. This is something that's returned by a function that does something asynchronously. Once the caller has possession of the deferred instance, it serves as a channel between the caller and the function. When the function is done with its asynchronous work, it notifies the caller and a callback function is run. There's a whole bunch of tricks we can perform with deferred instances, but we'll keep it straightforward here.

The job of the `query()` function we've implemented is to wrap the collection in a Lo-Dash wrapper and filter it using the `filter` argument. If the `sort` argument was provided, we sort the collection as well. The asynchronous work happens when we check the size of the collection. Note that we haven't actually executed any of the chained function calls yet, because we haven't called `value()`. If the collection contains more than 5,000 items, we use the Lo-Dash `defer()` function to clear the JavaScript call stack before executing `value()`. If the collection contains less items, we execute the filter immediately.

The result of calling `value()` is passed to the caller through the jQuery deferred instance, using the `resolve()` function. What's nice about this function is that it's always asynchronous to the caller. Even when we have smaller collections, it's still treated as asynchronous. The output illustrates when our randomized collection has more than 5,000 items, and the filter is deferred. When we see the `awaiting results` message, it means that the control had returned to the caller before the query was executed. This is the idea; since the collection is large, we let other things happen first in case the filter takes a while to complete.

Backbone

Unlike jQuery, Backbone is a library that's concerned with creating higher-level abstractions for the application. Things such as models, collections, and views are concepts that the Backbone programmer extends to provide seamless integration with the API data.

Backbone recognizes its own strengths and utilizes other libraries such as jQuery and Underscore to implement certain things such as fetching and saving data. This is a job well suited for jQuery as is rendering views in the DOM. For lower-level tasks, Backbone utilizes Underscore's capabilities. Because Backbone leverages these libraries, it's able to maintain a small code footprint. Moreover, since it follows simple patterns, it more or less stays out of the developer's way, letting them adapt the library to specific use cases.

There's an entire ecosystem surrounding Backbone, and Lo-Dash is a part of this ecosystem. Since it was originally conceived as a drop-in replacement for Underscore, Lo-Dash integrates closely with Backbone. In this section, we'll look at replacing Underscore in a Backbone application and extending Backbone's capabilities with functionality not found in Underscore.

Replacing Underscore.js

Backbone requires both jQuery and Underscore. Since it's wrapped as a UMD function, if we were to define Lo-Dash as an AMD module, it's quite simple to replace. Let's take a look at a RequireJS configuration that replaces Underscore with Lo-Dash:

```
require.config({
    paths: {
        jquery: 'lib/jquery.min',
        underscore: 'lib/lodash.backbone.min'
    },
    shim: {
        underscore: { exports: '_' }
    }
});
```

When the Backbone module loads, it looks for the `jquery` and the `underscore` modules, both of which we've provided here. You'll notice that the `underscore` module points to `lodash.backbone.min`. This is a special Lo-Dash build that contains only the functions required by Backbone. In other words, it doesn't have any extra stuff that Backbone doesn't use internally. Now let's define a simple model:

```
define([
```

```
        'underscore',
        'lib/backbone'
    ], function(_, Backbone) {
        return Backbone.Model.extend({
            parse: function(data) {
                return _.extend({
                    name: data.first + '' + data.last
                }, data);
            }
        });
    });
```

You can see that we require `underscore`, which is actually Lo-Dash, so we can use the `extend()` function. The Backbone model will also use Lo-Dash internally since it has the same Underscore requirement. Now let's use this model:

```
require([ 'modules/backbone-model' ], function(Model) {
    new Model({
        first: 'Lance',
        last: 'Newman'
    }, { parse: true }).toJSON();
    // → {name: "Lance Newman", first: "Lance", last: "Newman"}
});
```

The main reason you would drop Lo-Dash into Backbone like this is the improvement in speed and consistency Lo-Dash has over Underscore.

Full-featured Lo-Dash and Backbone

As our application grows in sophistication, we'll probably want more Lo-Dash functionality, despite this not being a strict requirement for Backbone. The alternative would be to replace Underscore with a full version of Lo-Dash. For this, we can use the AMD build of Lo-Dash. Here's a modified version of the RequireJS configuration:

```
require.config({
    paths: {
        jquery: 'lib/jquery.min',
        underscore: 'lib/lodash-amd/main'
    }
});
```

This is similar to the previous configuration, except that it doesn't require a shim to export the _ symbol and it points to the `main` Lo-Dash module. Let's redefine our model using this approach:

```
define([
    'lib/lodash-amd/object/assign',
    'lib/backbone'
], function(assign, Backbone) {
    return Backbone.Model.extend({
        parse: function(data) {
            return assign({
                name: data.first + '' + data.last
            }, data);
        }
    });
});
```

In this version of our model definition, we do not require Underscore. In fact, we only require one specific Lo-Dash function—`assign()`—in addition to Backbone. Mind you, Backbone will still load the entire Lo-Dash API.

Enhancing collections and models

If we require the full version of Lo-Dash, we can extend the capabilities of Backbone collections fairly easily. Let's define an extension module that extends Backbone collections with methods not found in Underscore:

```
define([
    'lib/backbone',
    'lib/lodash-amd/array/slice',
    'lib/lodash-amd/array/takeRight',
    'lib/lodash-amd/array/dropWhile'
], function(Backbone, slice, takeRight, dropWhile) {

    function extendCollection(func, name) {
        Backbone.Collection.prototype[name] = function() {
            var args = slice(arguments);
            args.unshift(this.models);
            return func.apply(null, args);
        }
    }

    extendCollection(takeRight, 'takeRight');
```

```
    extendCollection(dropWhile, 'dropWhile');

    return Backbone;
});
```

This module, whenever required, will extend the `Backbone.Collection` prototype with two new methods, `takeRight()` and `dropWhile()`. Note that it returns Backbone, so whenever we require Backbone, we can just use this module and get the extended version as a result. Let's see this extended collection in use:

```
require([
    'lib/lodash-amd/collection',
    'modules/backbone-extensions'
], function(_, Backbone) {

    function name(model) {
        return model.get('name');
    }

    var collection = new Backbone.Collection([
        { name: 'Frank' },
        { name: 'Darryl' },
        { name: 'Stacey' },
        { name: 'Robin' }
    ], { comparator: name });

    _.map(collection.takeRight(2), name );
    // → [ "Robin", "Stacey" ]

    _.map(collection.dropWhile(function(model, index, coll) {
        return index < (coll.length - 2);
    }), name);
    // → [ "Robin", "Stacey" ]

});
```

As you can see, the collection now has a `takeRight()` and a `dropWhile()` method —something that's easy to add since the functions are already implemented by Lo-Dash. We just need to glue the parts together, the same way as Backbone does with Underscore functions.

Node.js

In the closing section of this chapter, we'll turn our attention to writing Lo-Dash code for the backend. This of course means installing Lo-Dash as a Node.js package.

Installing the Lo-Dash package

Assuming you already have Node installed, since you had to do so in order to run the `grunt` command in the RequireJS examples, you should have an `npm` command on your system. If that's the case, installation is incredibly easy:

```
npm install -g lodash
```

This will install Lo-Dash globally, meaning it's accessible to any other Node project that wishes to use it. This is probably a good idea since Lo-Dash is a library after all. To verify that the installation was a success, you can run the following command:

```
node -e "require('lodash');"
```

If you see a long error message, it means that something went wrong at the time of installation. If it exists silently, you're all set.

Creating a simple command

To get our hands dirty with Node.js along with Lo-Dash development, let's create a simple command that sorts a comma-separated input:

```
var _ = require('lodash'),
    args = _(process.argv),
    input;

if (args.size() < 3) {
    console.error('Missing input');
    process.exit(1);
} else if (args.contains('-h')) {
    console.info('Sorts the comma-separated input');
    console.info('Use "-d" for descending order');
    process.exit(0);
}

input = _(process.argv[2].replace(/\s?(,)\s?/g, '$1').split(','))
    .sortBy();

if (args.contains('-d')) {
    input.reverse();
}

console.log(input.join(', '));
```

The `args` variable is a Lo-Dash wrapper that contains the command arguments as a value. We'll call `size()` and `contains()` on this wrapper to validate the input. A second wrapper is created and stored in the `input` variable. This is the comma-separated list, where we're splitting the string and removing any excess whitespaces. Then we call `sortBy()` to sort the list and optionally reverse the order if the `-d` flag was set. The string is then joined back together. Calling `join()` will actually execute the function call chain, and this is the output of the command.

Custom Lo-Dash builds

Another good reason to have Node.js installed is that you can install the `lodash-cli` package, which is the Lo-Dash build system. Using this tool, you can create custom builds on the fly and at a granular level. Right down to the function, you can specify what's included or what's excluded using the following command:

```
lodash modularize include=function
```

This will run an AMD build of Lo-Dash for us, only including what's necessary for functions in the `function` category.

Summary

This chapter focused on using Lo-Dash in the broader context of frontend development. Achieving modularity is made easier with technologies such as RequireJS. We looked at several ways to do this, and Lo-Dash has built-in support for these types on environments. We learned that Lo-Dash is a very focused library, helping the developer to write clean and efficient code while ignoring other things. The things that Lo-Dash isn't good at are nicely covered by other stable libraries such as jQuery and Backbone. We also wrote some Lo-Dash code that directly helps these libraries, both from a performance perspective and a functionality perspective.

We closed the chapter with a look at Node.js, and how it's possible to write Lo-Dash code for applications that run outside the browser. There's also a Node package that is used to build Lo-Dash and you can customize these builds to include whatever you like. Now that we've covered much ground on what you can do as a Lo-Dash programmer from the outside, let's take a look at the inside of Lo-Dash. Knowing how and why certain things are designed will better inform your decisions, in the interest of better performance.

8
Internal Design and Performance

The final chapter of this book looks at the internal design of key Lo-Dash components. All previous chapters focused on the external-facing aspects of the library. Now that we're well-versed in what's possible with Lo-Dash, it's time to see what's under the hood. This isn't an in-depth walkthrough of the Lo-Dash source code. The curious reader should by all means look at the code though. We will touch the most important pieces of the implementation of Lo-Dash. These are what make Lo-Dash perform not only fast but also predictably.

With these designs in mind, we'll spend the remaining sections of this chapter looking at some Lo-Dash code that could be improved. Understanding some of the design motivations will hopefully guide you in making your design decisions.

In this chapter, we will cover the following topics:

- Design principles
- Improving performance
- Lazy evaluation
- Caching things

Design principles

Lo-Dash had some fairly modest goals in the beginning. Underscore appealed to the masses because of the problems it solved and because its API was coherent and easy to use. Lo-Dash's creator, John-David Dalton, wanted to prove that it was possible to implement a great API, such as Underscore's, while delivering consistency and performance across browsers. Additionally, Lo-Dash has the freedom to implement new features that aren't welcomed by Underscore.

In order to prove his point, John-David had to establish some guiding design principles. Some of the founding principles are still around today, while others have morphed into something else to better support programmers who use the library and contribute to it. Lo-Dash is nothing if not adaptable to change.

Function compilation to base functions

The earlier versions of Lo-Dash utilized a technique called **function compilation**. This means that there were templates of a skeleton function. Then Lo-Dash would fill them and create function instances on the fly. These were then exposed through the API. The nice thing about this approach is that it is easy to implement a ton of variability for one function without the need to implement several versions of that function. Being able to implement generic functions like this while keeping the code size small meant that Lo-Dash was able to tackle all sorts of different use cases, from both a performance perspective and a bug-fixing/consistency perspective. However, this approach was holding Lo-Dash back in two ways.

The first issue with function compilation is the readability of the code—something so dynamic isn't all that approachable by developers. This aspect of open source goes out the window—you don't get folks reviewing code by scaring them off. The second issue is that JavaScript engines are continually improving their ability to optimize JavaScript code as it runs. This is also known as **just-in-time (JIT)** optimization. So between now and the time that Lo-Dash was first conceived, browser vendors have come a long way. In such a short time, these improvements weren't being fully utilized by Lo-Dash and its approach of function compilation.

In recent versions of Lo-Dash (2.4 and 3.0 in particular), the function compilation approach has been replaced with **base functions**. In other words, base functions are generic components, used by several publicly-facing functions. The earlier versions of the library shied away from abstractions due to the fear that unnecessary indirection would mean performance penalty. While it's true that abstractions do incur an overhead cost, it turns out that helping the browser perform JIT optimizations outweighs this cost.

This doesn't mean that Lo-Dash has abandoned all caution of abstraction overhead. The implementation is quite clever and readable, which solves earlier issues of comprehending the source. A given base function is probably used in several places, which reduces repetitive code. What's more important is the way the base functions are structured. A given function that's exposed through the API will do some initial work to make sense of the arguments that were passed. Essentially, this is the preparation so that more exact arguments can be passed to the base function. This results in better predictability for the JavaScript engine. The cost of calling a base function is often negated, especially when the same call is made frequently—the engine will often inline the function to where it's called.

So what's the implication here for Lo-Dash programmers? Nothing really. The way these internal base functions are structured and used should not impact your code at all. This, however, should give some insight into how Lo-Dash is able to evolve quickly, based on developer feedback and changing JavaScript technologies.

Optimizing for the common case

This principle, **optimize for the common case**, has been with Lo-Dash from day one. Sure, subtle implementation details have evolved, but the underlying idea remains intact and this will likely always be the case. Think of this as the golden rule in Lo-Dash (the unofficial rule). Just as the Linux kernel development has a golden rule, called *don't break user space*, think of *optimize for the common case* as something to always strive for.

Take the base function approach that's now used in favor of function compilation. We can choose which base function to call based on the arguments the user has supplied. For example, a function that accepts a collection could use a base function that works only with arrays. It's optimized for arrays. So, when the function that accepts a collection is called, it checks whether it's dealing with an array or not. If it is, it'll use the faster base function. Here's an illustration of the pattern using pseudo-JavaScript:

```
function apiCollectionFunction(collection) {
    if (_.isArray(collection)) {
        return baseArray(collection);
    } else {
        return baseGeneric(collection)
    }
}
```

The common path is the first path that's tested. The `baseArray()` function that is executed is generic enough and used frequently enough to get special treatment from the JIT. The strategy is to assume that the common case is passing an array. The assumption isn't arbitrary either; it's benchmarked against typical use cases during development. The worst case is when we're dealing with a string or when a plain object isn't slow, necessarily, it's just not optimized. So these slower calls, as infrequent as they are, will be offset by the optimized calls that happen all the time.

The common case can even be tiered. That is, your function is thrown one of several cases when called, and all of those possibilities have an order to their frequency. For example, if the most common case isn't met, what's the next most common case? And so on. The effect of this technique pushes the uncommon code down towards the bottom of the function. On its own, this doesn't have a huge impact on performance, but when every function in the library consistently follows the same common case optimization techniques, the impact is huge.

Loops are simple

Lo-Dash uses a lot of loops in its code. That's because there's a lot of iterating over collections. It's also because Lo-Dash does not use certain native functions that would otherwise negate the need for a loop. This is the opposite of the stance Underscore.js takes on this matter. It prefers the native methods whenever they're available. The logic being the JavaScript library shouldn't have to worry about iteration performance. Instead, the browser vendor should improve the native method performance.

This approach makes sense, especially when the side effect is writing less code. However, Lo-Dash doesn't rely on the browser vendor to deliver performance. We can get better performance out of simple `while` loops and this will likely continue in the foreseeable future. Native methods are undoubtedly faster than unoptimized JavaScript code, but they aren't able to perform the same kind of optimizations as we're able to when using pure JavaScript.

> Lo-Dash is a strategic animal. It doesn't like to rely on certain native JavaScript methods, but it relies heavily on the JIT abilities of any given JavaScript engine for performance, cost balancing in action.

Lo-Dash also doesn't like to rely on `for` loops—`while` loops are preferred. The `for` loop is useful when used to iterate over collections, thus enhancing code readability. Under these simple circumstances, trying to use a `while` loop is just cumbersome. Even though the `while` loop does have a slight performance edge over the `for` loop, it's not really all that noticeable. The performance difference is noticeable in the case of several large collections that are frequently iterated over. This is the common case that Lo-Dash accounts for. Consider the following code:

```
var collection = _.range(10000000),
    length = collection.length,
    i = 0;

console.time('for');
for (; i < length; i++) {
    collection[i];
}
console.timeEnd('for');

i = 0;

console.time('while');
```

```
while (++i < length) {
    collection[i];
}
console.timeEnd('while');
// →
// for: 13.459ms
// while: 10.670ms
```

The difference between the two loops is hardly perceptible. Probably a couple of years ago, the lead the `while` loop had over `for` may have been wider, which is one reason Lo-Dash is still using `while` loops everywhere. Another reason is consistency. Since the `while` loop is nearly identical wherever it's implemented in Lo-Dash, you can expect its performance to be predictable throughout. This is especially true given that there's not a mixture of `while` loops, `for` loops, and native JavaScript methods. Sometimes, predictable performance is better than *sometimes it's faster, but I can never be sure.*

Callbacks and function binding

Callbacks are used everywhere in Lo-Dash, both internally and as arguments of API functions. So it's important that these functions get executed with as little overhead as possible. The big culprit that slows down these function calls is the `this` context, that is, the context that the function is bound to. If there's no context to consider, then there's clearly less overhead involved, especially considering that these callback functions typically get called once per iteration if the function is operating on a collection.

If there's a specific context for the callback function, then we have to use `call()` to call the function, since it allows us to set the context. Or if there are an unknown number of arguments, we use the `apply()` function, passing the context and the arguments as an array. This is especially slow if executed iteratively. To help combat these performance hurdles, Lo-Dash uses a base function to help construct callback functions.

This function is used anywhere where there's a callback function passed as an argument. The first step is to use this function to build a potentially wrapped callback function. This initial examination is worth the cost because of the potential savings when it has to be called iteratively. Here's a rough idea of how this function works:

```
function baseCallback(func, thisArg, argCount) {
    if (!thisArg) {
        return func;
    }

    if (alreadyBound(func)) {
```

```
            return func;
        }

        if (argCount == 1) {
            return function(collection) {
                return func.call(thisArg, collection);
            }
        }

        return function() {
            return func.apply(thisArg, arguments);
        }
    }
```

This is a gross simplification of what `baseCallback()` is really doing, but the general pattern is accurate. The most common cases that build a callback function are checked first. The uncommon, slower cases are pushed to the bottom. For example, if there's no `thisArg`, we don't have to bind the function; it can just be returned. The next case that is checked is whether or not the function has already been bound. If it has been, then the `thisArg` value is ignored and the function is returned. If neither of these checks passes and the `argCount` argument is supplied, we can use `call()`, supplying the exact number of arguments. The preceding pseudocode shows the case of only a single argument, but in reality, it checks for several exact argument counts.

The uncommon case is when `thisArg` is supplied, meaning we have to bind the function and we don't know how many arguments are there. So, we use `apply()`, the slowest scenario. Other cases `baseCallback()` is able to handle include a string or a plain object being passed as `func` instead of a function instance. For such cases, there are specific callback functions that get returned and this is also checked for early on since it's a common case.

The `alreadyBound()` function is something made up for brevity. Lo-Dash knows whether a function is already bound or not by looking at the metadata for that function. In this context, metadata refers to data that's attached to the function by Lo-Dash, but is completely transparent to the developer. For example, many callbacks will track data about the frequency with which they are called. If the function becomes *hot*, Lo-Dash will treat it differently than callbacks that aren't executed frequently.

Improving performance

Just because Lo-Dash is designed from the ground up for optimal performance, it doesn't mean there are no basic modifications we can make to our Lo-Dash code to improve performance. In fact, we can sometimes borrow some Lo-Dash design principles and apply them directly to our code that utilizes Lo-Dash.

Changing the operation order

Using a Lo-Dash wrapper around a value, such as an array, lets us chain together many operations on that value. As we saw in *Chapter 6, Application Building Blocks*, a wrapper has many advantages over stitching together, piecemeal, several statements that call Lo-Dash functions. For example, the end result is often more concise and readable code. The different orders in which we call these operations in a chain can yield the same result and yet have different performance implications. Let's look at three different approaches to filtering a collection that get us the same result:

```
var collection = _.map(_.range(100), function(item) {
    return {
        id: item,
        enabled: !!_.random()
    };
});

var cnt = 1000;

console.time('first');
while (--cnt) {
    _(collection)
        .filter('enabled')
        .filter(function(item) {
            return item.id > 75;
        })
        .value();
}
```

```
console.timeEnd('first');

cnt = 1000;

console.time('second');
while (--cnt) {
    _(collection)
        .filter(function(item) {
            return item.id > 75;
        })
        .filter('enabled')
        .value();
}
console.timeEnd('second');

cnt = 1000;

console.time('third');
while (--cnt) {
    _(collection)
        .filter(function(item) {
            return item.enabled && item.id > 75;
        })
        .value();
}
console.timeEnd('third');
// →
// first: 13.368ms
// second: 6.263ms
// third: 3.198ms
```

The `collection` array is quite straightforward. It contains `100` items and each item is an object with two properties. The first is a numerical ID. The second is a random Boolean value. The goal is to filter out anything that's not `enabled` and anything with an `id` value that is less than `75`.

The first approach builds a chain consisting of two `filter()` calls. The first `filter()` call removes any disabled items. The second approach removes anything with an `id` property whose value is less than `75`. However, the ordering of these filtering operations isn't optimal. You might have noticed that there are a large number of items removed based on their `id` value. This is due to the nature of the filter and the dataset we're dealing with.

Any calls made to `filter()` mean that a linear iteration takes place over the collection. With the first approach, there are two calls made to `filter()`, which means that we'll have to iterate linearly over the collection twice. Given what we now know about the collection data and what the filter is looking for, we can optimize the ordering of the filter calls. This is a simple change. We first filter by `id` and then by the `enabled` property. The result is a noticeable boost in performance because the second call to `filter()` has to iterate over far fewer items.

The third approach takes things a step further and removes an iteration completely. Since both filter conditions are checked in the `filter()` callback function, there's no need to iterate over any collection item twice.

> Of course, the trade-off here is more complexity in the given callback function. Keep this in mind if your application does lots of filtering, because you'll want to avoid defining highly specialized callback functions that serve a single purpose. It's generally a better idea to keep your functions small and generic. The second approach strikes a good balance. These types of optimizations don't often happen upfront, so wait until the common case reveals itself before trying to optimize for it.

Sorting and indexing collections

If the order of the collection is an important factor in the application you're developing, you can introduce tweaks that take advantage of its importance. These tweaks include maintaining the sort order. There's really no point in re-sorting collections every time you need to render it. Rather, it's better to sort the collection once and then maintain its order by inserting new items in the correct place. Lo-Dash has the `sortedIndex()` function, which helps find the proper insertion point for new items. In fact, it performs a binary search and is much faster than a linear search through the collection.

For faster filtering operations, we can borrow the `sortedIndex()` function. If we have a sorted collection, there's really no need to filter items using a linear search, which performs rather poorly in the worst case. Let's introduce a new `mixin` function that performs the same job as the `filter()` function but is optimized for sorted collections:

```
_.mixin({ sortedFilter: function(collection, value, iteratee) {
    iteratee = _.callback(iteratee);
    var index = _.sortedIndex(collection, value, iteratee),
        result = [],
        item;
    while (true) {
```

```
            item = collection[index++];
            if (_.isEqual(iteratee(item), iteratee(value))) {
                result.push(item);
            } else {
                break;
            }
        }
        return result;
}});

var collection = _.map(_.range(100), function(item) {
    return {
        id: item,
        age: _.random(50)
    };
});

var shuffled = _.shuffle(collection),
    sorted = _.sortBy(shuffled, 'age');

console.time('shuffled');
console.log(_.filter(shuffled, { age: 25 }));
console.timeEnd('shuffled');
// →
// [
//   { id: 63, age: 25 },
//   { id: 6, age: 25 },
//   { id: 89, age: 25 }
// ]
// shuffled: 4.936ms

console.time('sorted');
console.log(_.sortedFilter(sorted, { age: 25 }, 'age'));
console.timeEnd('sorted');
// →
// [
//   { id: 63, age: 25 },
//   { id: 6, age: 25 },
//   { id: 89, age: 25 }
// ]
// sorted: 0.831ms
```

The new function we've introduced—`sortedFilter()`—is faster than the `filter()` function. Again, this is because we don't have to rely on a linear search, since the collection is sorted. Instead, the `sortedIndex()` function is used to find what we're looking for. It uses a binary search, which means that with larger collections, there are a large number of items that aren't checked. The end result is fewer CPU cycles and faster execution time.

Our `sortedFilter()` implementation, thanks largely to `sortedIndex()`, isn't all that complicated. The binary search gets us the insertion point to insert the new item, but we're not actually inserting anything. We're just looking for it. There could be several items that match our criteria, or there could be none. This is where we iterate over the collection, using the insertion index as a starting point. We now have to explicitly check the values using `isEqual()` and build the result array. Since the collection is sorted, we know to stop and return when items stop matching the filter criteria.

> Always take care to validate your code for correctness when improving Lo-Dash functions for performance purposes. The easiest way to do this is to set up a number of automated tests that compare the output of the Lo-Dash function with that of your faster variant. This allows you to throw all kinds of edge cases at your code before you get too excited about your newly found speed. Lo-Dash takes care of a lot of edge cases, so make sure you don't sidestep safety in favor of performance.

Another technique in speeding up filtering operations on collections is to index them. This means creating a new data structure that uses keys to look for common items in the collection. This is another way to avoid the costly linear search in large collections. Here's an example that uses `groupBy()` to index a collection for a fast search of items using common filtering criteria:

```
var collection = _.map(_.range(100), function(item) {
    return {
        id: item,
        age: _.random(50),
        enabled: !!_.random()
    };
});

var indexed = _.groupBy(collection, function(item) {
    return +item.enabled * item.age;
});

console.time('where');
```

```
console.log(_.where(collection, { age: 25, enabled: true }));
console.timeEnd('where');
// →
// [
//   { id: 23, age: 25, enabled: true },
//   { id: 89, age: 25, enabled: true }
// ]
// where: 5.528ms

console.time('indexed');
console.log(indexed[25] || []);
console.timeEnd('indexed');
// →
// [
//   { id: 23, age: 25, enabled: true },
//   { id: 89, age: 25, enabled: true }
// ]
// indexed: 0.712ms
```

The indexed approach takes much less time than the `where()` approach to look for the same items. This approach is useful when there are several instances of the same filter throughout your application. The `indexed` variable holds the indexed version of the collection. The index is created using the `groupBy()` function. It takes an array as the input and produces an object. The index keys are the object keys, and the callback passed to `groupBy()` is responsible for generating these keys. The function returns the key value, and if the key already exists, the item is added to that key.

The idea is that we want items indexed by their `age` property value, and by whether or not they're `enabled`. We use a neat little trick here to do that. The `enabled` property is converted to a positive integer and multiplied by the `age` value. So any disabled items will be indexed under `0`, where nobody looks. Now you can see that looking for the items in the `indexed` object yields the same results as the `where()` filter. With the latter approach, we're doing a simple object access operation rather than iterating over a collection and performing several operations.

> While the speedups here are quite impressive, be sure to consider the update frequency for items in this collection. If you think about it, the indexed version is really just a cache of common filter results. So if the collection is never updated, you're good to go assuming you're okay with the one-time payment of actually indexing the collection.

Bound and unbound callbacks

Lo-Dash embraces callback functions and does a really good job of optimizing the way they're called. For example, it avoids using `call()` and `apply()` when there's no `this` context necessary, and this is for a good reason—these calls are a lot slower than unbound function calls. So when we're writing our application that utilizes Lo-Dash callback functions, we have the option to provide context to each of these callbacks as they're applied to collections. Take the time to weigh the trade-offs before coding functions in this way.

Binding our functions to a context is convenient when we want to use the same function in a different context. This isn't always necessary and it depends largely on the overall design of our code. If we have tons of objects that our callbacks need to access, the `this` context is pretty convenient. We might even have a single application object that is used to access other objects, and so on. If that's the case, we'll definitely need a way to pass this object to our callback functions. This could mean binding the `this` context, accessing the object through function closure, or creating a partial function for our callback.

None of these options are particularly performance friendly. Therefore, if we find that our callbacks are in constant need of access to some object, it might make sense to define it in a callback function, instead of defining it as a variable. The following code illustrates this idea:

```
function callback(item) {
    return _.extend({
        version: this.version
    }, item);
}

function unbound(item) {
    return _.extend({
        version: 2.0
    }, item);
}

var cnt - 1000,
    app = { version: 2.0 },
    boundCallback = _.callback(callback, app),
    collection = _.map(_.range(1000), function(item) {
```

```
            return { id: item };
        });

    console.time('bound');
    while (--cnt) {
        _.map(collection, boundCallback);
    }
    console.timeEnd('bound');

    cnt = 1000;

    console.time('unbound');
    while (--cnt) {
        _.map(collection, unbound);
    }
    console.timeEnd('unbound');
    // →
    // bound: 662.418ms
    // unbound: 594.799ms
```

We can see that the unbound callback function will generally outperform the bound callback function. What's important to note here is the approach. The `bound()` function is bound to a specific context with the call to `map()`. This is because it needs something from the application object. The `unbound()` function, instead of relying on some external instance, will declare the variable itself. So we will get what we need for the callback without the need to bind to a specific callback function.

At first, this may seem like a counterintuitive approach to defining application-level variables inside a callback function. Well, it boils down to the rest of your code. Do you have a lot of callback functions that require access to this data? If you put this callback function in an easy-to-locate place in your source tree, then it's really not all that different from modifying a variable.

> Switching from bound to unbound functions doesn't yield a huge performance gain when there are just a handful of callback functions. Even if there are lots of functions, it's fine to have several bound functions without impacting performance. The idea of this section is to keep you on the lookout for functions that are *needlessly* bound to a context. Fix them where you can if they don't have a noticeable impact on your design.

Lazy evaluation

With the introduction of Lo-Dash 3.0, some functions use a **lazy evaluation** to compute their results. This simply means that the items in a given collection aren't iterated over until they're actually needed. It's figuring out when they're needed that is the tricky part. For example, just calling a single Lo-Dash function doesn't invoke any lazy evaluation mechanism. However, operations that are chained together could certainly benefit from this approach, in certain circumstances. For example, when we're only taking 10 items from the result, there's no need to iterate over the entire collection further up the chain.

To get an idea of what a lazy evaluation looks like, let's write some code to utilize it. There's nothing explicit to be done. The lazy mechanism happens transparently, behind the scenes, depending on which operations make up our chain and what order they're called in:

```
var collection = _.range(10);

_(collection)
    .reject(function(item) {
        console.log('checking ' + item);
        return item % 2;
    })
    .map(function(item) {
        console.log('mapping ' + item);
        return item * item;
     })
    .value();
// →
// checking 1
// checking 2
// mapping 2
// checking 3
```

Here, our chain is composed of two functions—`reject()` and `map()`. Since `reject()` is called first, Lo-Dash makes it a lazy wrapper. This means that when `value()` is called, things are done a bit differently. Rather than running each function to completion, the lazy functions in the chain are asked for a value. For example, `reject()` doesn't run until `map()` asks it for a value. When it does, `reject()` will run till it produces a value. We can actually see this behavior in the output. The `reject()` function is checking item `1`, which gets rejected. It then moves on to item `2`, which passes the test. This is then passed to `map()`. Then item `3` is checked, and so on.

The two function calls are interleaved and this property can extend upward through many functions in a more complicated chain. The advantage is that if these functions are too expensive to run through an entire collection, they generally don't have to. They'll execute only when asked to execute. Let's see this concept in action:

```
var collection = _.range(1000000).reverse();

console.time('motivated');
_.take(_.filter(collection, function(item) {
    return !(item % 10);
}), 10);
console.timeEnd('motivated');

console.time('lazy');
_(collection)
    .filter(function(item) {
        return !(item % 10);
    })
    .take(100)
    .value();
console.timeEnd('lazy');
// →
// motivated: 8.454ms
// lazy: 0.889ms
```

You can see that the lazy approach takes much less time than the motivated approach, even though it is taking `100` results and the latter is taking only `10`. The reason is simple—the collection is large and the entire thing is filtered using the motivated approach. The lazy approach uses far fewer iterations.

Caching things

The best way to improve the performance of an operation is to not perform it—at least not twice, or worse, hundreds or thousands of times. Repeating costly computations is an unnecessary waste of CPU cycles and can be avoided by caching the results. The `memoize()` function helps us here, by caching the results of the called function for later use. However, caching has its own overheads and pitfalls to be aware of. Let's start by taking a look at idempotent functions—these always produce the same output when given the same input arguments:

```
function primeFactors(number) {
    var factors = [],
        divisor = 2;

    while (number > 1) {
```

```
        while (number % divisor === 0) {
            factors.push(divisor);
            number /= divisor;
        }
        divisor += 1;
        if (divisor * divisor > number) {
            if (number > 1) {
                factors.push(number);
            }
            break;
        }
    }
    return factors;
}

var collection = _.map(_.range(10000), function() {
        return _.random(1000000, 1000010);
    }),
    primes = _.memoize(primeFactors);

console.time('primes');
_.each(collection, function(item) {
    primeFactors(item);
});
console.timeEnd('primes');

console.time('cached');
_.each(collection, function(item) {
    primes(item);
});
console.timeEnd('cached');
// →
// primes: 17.564ms
// cached: 4.930ms
```

The `primeFactors()` function returns an array of prime factors of the given number. It has to do a fair amount of work to compute the returned array. There is nothing that hogs the CPU for any substantial amount of time, but nonetheless, it's work—work that yields the same result for a given input. Idempotent functions such as these are good candidates for memoization. This is easy to do with the `memoize()` function and we use this function to generate the `primes()` function. Also note that the cache key is the first argument, which is nice and easy here because it's the only input we're interested in caching.

> It's important to take into consideration the amount of overhead involved with looking up cached items. It's not a lot, but it's there. Often, this overhead outweighs the value of caching the results in the first place. The preceding code is a case of testing with a relatively large collection. As that collection size shrinks, so does the performance gain.

While it's nice to cache the results of idempotent functions because you never have to worry about invalidating that cache, let's look at a more common use case:

```
function mapAges(collection) {
    return _.map(collection, 'age');
}

var collection = _.map(_.range(100), function(item) {
        return {
            id: item,
            age: _.random(50)
        };
    }),
    ages = _.memoize(mapAges, function(collection) {
        if (_.has(collection, 'mapAges')) {
            return collection.mapAges;
        } else {
            collection.mapAges = _.uniqueId();
        }
    }),
    cnt = 1000;

console.time('mapAges');
while (--cnt) {
    _.reduce(mapAges(collection), function(result, item) {
        return result + item;
    }) / collection.length;
}
console.timeEnd('mapAges');

cnt = 1000;

console.time('ages');
while (--cnt) {
```

```
    _.reduce(ages(collection), function(result, item) {
        return result + item;
    }) / collection.length;
}
console.timeEnd('ages');
// →
// mapAges: 6.878ms
// ages: 3.535ms
```

Here we're caching the result of mapping a collection to a different representation. In other words, we're mapping the `age` property. This mapping operation can be costly if it's repeated throughout the application. So we use the `memoize()` function to cache the result of mapping the age values, resulting in the `ages()` function. However, there's still the issue of looking up the cached collection—we need a key resolution function. The one we've provided is quite simple. It assigns a unique identifier to the `mapAges` property of the collection. The next time `ages()` is called, this identifier is found and the cached copy is looked up.

We can see that not having to map the collection again and again saves CPU cycles. And this is a simple mapping; other mappings with callback functions can be costlier and much more elaborate than simply plucking a value.

> Of course, this code assumes that this collection is constant and never changes. If you're building a large application with lots of moving parts, static collections like these are actually quite common. If the collection, or items in the collection for that matter, change frequently throughout its lifetime, you have to start thinking about invalidating the cache. It's probably not worth caching maps or other transformations for temperamental collections because, apart from naming things, cache invalidation is the toughest of all problems in programming.

Summary

In this chapter, we introduced some of the influences that guide the design and implementation of Lo-Dash. Earlier versions of the library opted for function compilation, building the functions on the fly to best handle performance and other variations from environment to environment. Recent versions have traded this approach for common base functions. Function compilation avoided some of the indirection associated with base functions. However, modern browsers have a JIT optimizer. It is better able to optimize base functions. Besides, the code is much more readable with base functions.

The golden rule of the implementation of Lo-Dash is optimization for the common case. You'll see this rule in action all over Lo-Dash, and it is the key factor in its superior performance. In any given function, the most common case is heavily optimized first, pushing the uncommon cases towards the end of the function. Callbacks are used everywhere in Lo-Dash, so it's important that they're able to perform predictably. The base callback machinery takes care of this for us and serves as a great example of optimizing for the common case.

We then looked at some techniques used to optimize our Lo-Dash code, following the design principles of Lo-Dash in most cases. Changing the order of chained operations in a Lo-Dash wrapper can eliminate needless iterations. Working with sorted collections can have a dramatic impact on filter performance. Lazy evaluation is a concept recently introduced to Lo-Dash, and it allows us to work with large collections without necessarily iterating over the entire collection. Lastly, we looked at some scenarios where caching could help boost performance, especially where the computations are expensive.

With that said, you're all set. Throughout this book, we learned and implemented concept after concept, starting with what you get out of the box in Lo-Dash, and wrapping up with how to go faster. Along the way, we looked at the most common usage patterns used to write solid Lo-Dash code. By now, it should be clear how everything in Lo-Dash relates to everything else, from the conceptual to the low-level function calls. As with any other library, there are a dozen or more ways of doing something in Lo-Dash. I hope you're now well-equipped to do it the best way.

Index

D

E

F

K

L

M

N

O

Thank you for buying
Lo-Dash Essentials

About Packt Publishing

Packt, pronounced 'packed', published its first book, *Mastering phpMyAdmin for Effective MySQL Management*, in April 2004, and subsequently continued to specialize in publishing highly focused books on specific technologies and solutions.

Our books and publications share the experiences of your fellow IT professionals in adapting and customizing today's systems, applications, and frameworks. Our solution-based books give you the knowledge and power to customize the software and technologies you're using to get the job done. Packt books are more specific and less general than the IT books you have seen in the past. Our unique business model allows us to bring you more focused information, giving you more of what you need to know, and less of what you don't.

Packt is a modern yet unique publishing company that focuses on producing quality, cutting-edge books for communities of developers, administrators, and newbies alike. For more information, please visit our website at `www.packtpub.com`.

About Packt Open Source

In 2010, Packt launched two new brands, Packt Open Source and Packt Enterprise, in order to continue its focus on specialization. This book is part of the Packt Open Source brand, home to books published on software built around open source licenses, and offering information to anybody from advanced developers to budding web designers. The Open Source brand also runs Packt's Open Source Royalty Scheme, by which Packt gives a royalty to each open source project about whose software a book is sold.

Writing for Packt

We welcome all inquiries from people who are interested in authoring. Book proposals should be sent to `author@packtpub.com`. If your book idea is still at an early stage and you would like to discuss it first before writing a formal book proposal, then please contact us; one of our commissioning editors will get in touch with you.

We're not just looking for published authors; if you have strong technical skills but no writing experience, our experienced editors can help you develop a writing career, or simply get some additional reward for your expertise.

[PACKT] open source
community experience distilled
PUBLISHING

Mastering KnockoutJS

ISBN: 978-1-78398-100-7 Paperback: 270 pages

Use and extend Knockout to deliver feature-rich, modern web applications

1. Customize Knockout to add functionality and integrate with third-party libraries.
2. Create full web applications using binding preprocessors, Node preprocessors, and the Knockout Punches library.
3. In a step-by-step manner, explore the Knockout ecosystem by looking at popular plugins as well as the Durandal Framework.

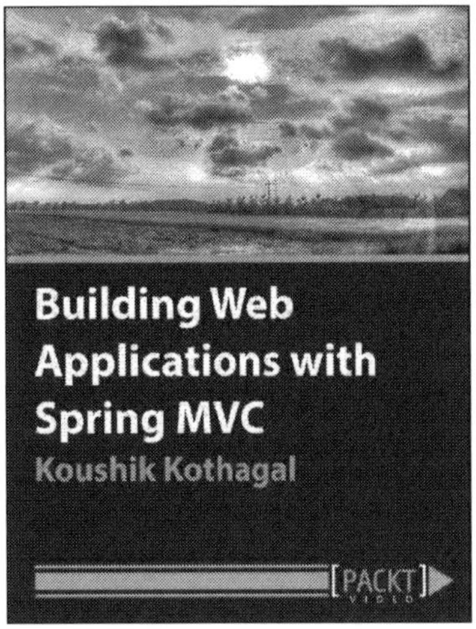

Building Web Applications with Spring MVC [Video]

ISBN: 978-1-78328-653-9 Duration: 03:13 hrs

Build dynamic and powerful server-side web applications in Java using Spring MVC

1. Implement Spring MVC controllers that handle user requests, return HTML responses, and handle errors.
2. Provide locale and theme support for web applications as well as build sturdy RESTful web services.
3. A practical guide that demonstrates building Spring MVC applications using an example of an online e-commerce chocolate store.

Please check **www.PacktPub.com** for information on our titles

45446308R00131

Made in the USA
San Bernardino, CA
09 February 2017